Alice's Daughter *explores the journey of an Aboriginal woman placed in a remote mission settlement in WA at the age of three years. Despite cultural deprivation, dispossession institutionalisation and isolation she refused to settle for such lifestyle. Upon embarking on a successful quest to reclaim her Aboriginality, family and mother she developed into a strong Aboriginal woman, poet, storyteller, artist, singer and songwriter. This book is an exciting read.*

Emeritus Professor MaryAnn Bin-Sallik AO

This work brings forward a number of dark stories and memories from behind a series of tragic walls that had been built to conquer and hold silent the indomitable spirit of a young Aboriginal woman. Rhonda Collard may have been pushed down and held down, but she fought back and rose up against those that sought to defeat her. From the harsh, dusty country of her tribal nation, we follow Rhonda's journey to the bitumen streets of this nation's cities and we weep when we share her pain, but then rejoice when we laugh within her songs.

Sam Watson, Wanjiburrah Man, Southern Queensland Country

First published in 2017
by Aboriginal Studies Press

© Text, Rhonda Collard-Spratt and Jacki Ferro 2017
© Poetry and artwok, Rhonda Collard-Spratt 2017

All rights reserved. No part of this book may be reproduced or transmitted in any form or by any means, electronic or mechanical, including photocopying, recording or by any information storage and retrieval system, without prior permission in writing from the publisher. The Australian *Copyright Act 1968* (the Act) allows a maximum of one chapter or 10 per cent of this book, whichever is the greater, to be photocopied by any educational institution for its education purposes provided that the educational institution (or body that administers it) has given a remuneration notice to Copyright Agency Limited (CAL) under the Act.

Aboriginal Studies Press
is the publishing arm of the
Australian Institute of Aboriginal
and Torres Strait Islander Studies.
GPO Box 553, Canberra, ACT 2601
Phone: (61 2) 6246 1183
Fax: (61 2) 6261 4288
Email: asp@aiatsis.gov.au
Web: www.aiatsis.gov.au/asp/about.html

ISBN: 9781925302936 (pb)
ISBN: 9781925302943 (epub)
ISBN: 978125302516 (ebook PDF)
ISBN: 9781925302509 (Kindle)

National Library of Australia
Cataloguing-In-Publication data is
available at www.trove.nla.gov.au

Printed in Australia by SOS Print Group

Front cover: 'Treasured Memories' (2015); Rhonda aged sixteen.

Back cover artwork: 'Coming Together' (2011). This artwork is about coming together as people, and respecting each other's differences; taking the time to sit around and hear each other's stories without judgement. It's about finding that we are the same in many ways, and trying to bridge that gap between us on a cultural level. It's about understanding each other's different journeys in life and how that has shaped us. Listen with your heart then go on your different path from our sacred circle where we have passed on what we've learnt from each other.

Aboriginal and Torres Strait Islander readers are respectfully advised that this book contains names and photographs of deceased persons, and culturally sensitive material.

Alice's Daughter **also includes original government records containing language that may disturb and offend some readers. It includes words and terms that were acceptable at the time of their usage, but are no longer appropriate today. The authors apologise for any upset or sadness caused.**

Some names and identifying characteristics have been changed to protect personal privacy.

Every effort has been made to contact copyright owners. If a photograph appears in this book without due acknowledgment, please contact the publishers.

A glossary of Aboriginal language and Australian English terms can be found at the end of the book.

Readers should also note that some chapters refer to incidents that could trigger past trauma or cause distress. You can find links to health resources and helplines at https://www.1800respect.org.au/telephone-and-online-counselling/.

Alice's Daughter

Lost mission child

Rhonda Collard-Spratt with Jacki Ferro

In honour of my mother
and all Carnarvon mission kids who share this history with me.
For my precious grandchildren, Latisha,
Michael and Ebony Davies.
— Rhonda Collard-Spratt

Contents

List of poetry

List of images and artwork

(see between pages 80 and 81)

Images

Transcribed letters

Facsimiles

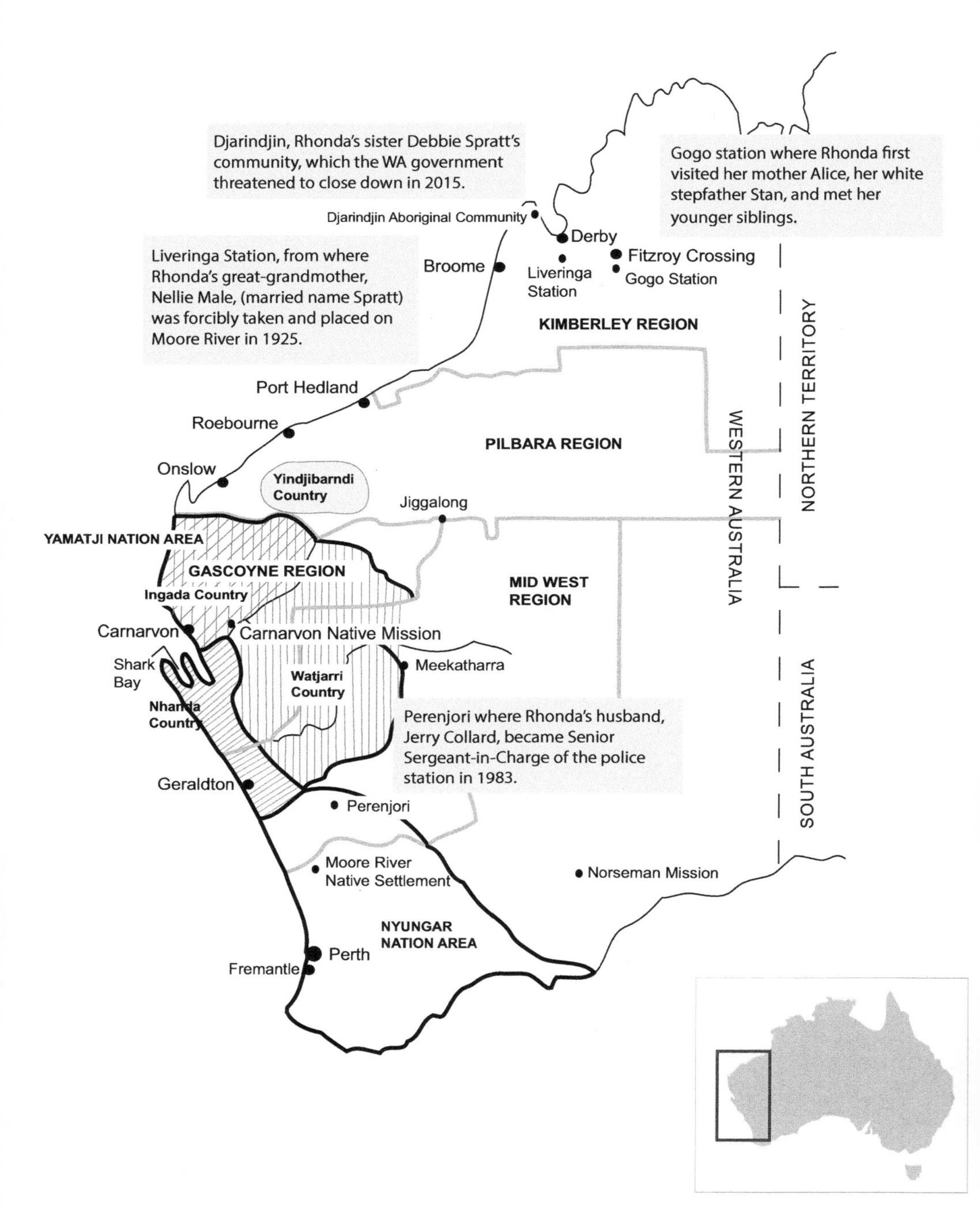
Djarindjin, Rhonda's sister Debbie Spratt's community, which the WA government threatened to close down in 2015.
Gogo station where Rhonda first visited her mother Alice, her white stepfather Stan, and met her younger siblings.
Djarindjin Aboriginal Community
Derby
Liveringa Station, from where Rhonda's great-grandmother, Nellie Male, (married name Spratt) was forcibly taken and placed on Moore River in 1925.
Broome
Liveringa Station
Fitzroy Crossing
Gogo Station
KIMBERLEY REGION
NORTHERN TERRITORY
Port Hedland
Roebourne
PILBARA REGION
WESTERN AUSTRALIA
Onslow
Yindjibarndi Country
Jiggalong
YAMATJI NATION AREA
GASCOYNE REGION
MID WEST REGION
Ingada Country
Carnarvon
Carnarvon Native Mission
Shark Bay
Meekatharra
Watjarri Country
Nhanda Country
SOUTH AUSTRALIA
Perenjori where Rhonda's husband, Jerry Collard, became Senior Sergeant-in-Charge of the police station in 1983.
Geraldton
Perenjori
Moore River Native Settlement
Norseman Mission
NYUNGAR NATION AREA
Perth
Fremantle

Map of the primary area and places referred to in this book.

Acknowledgments

To Jerry, thanks for the memories. To our children, John and Lisa, it's an honour to have you in my life. You are the reason I live. And to Debbie, you are the beat of my heart. My heartfelt thanks I give to Jacki, who has given me her precious time to journey with me as we worked side by side in telling my story. We have shared many emotions during this time — we have sung songs, laughed, hugged and cried as my memories came alive through her fingertips.
— Rhonda Collard-Spratt

Thanks to my beautiful husband Vito who said, 'You need to write this.'

Thanks too to my parents, Brian and Teresa Hauff, who always encourage and believe in me. Rhonda, my greatest thanks to you for sharing your most intimate stories with me. I am blessed to know you, and to call you my friend.
— Jacki Ferro

The authors respectfully acknowledge the following publication in which photographs of Rhonda's life at Carnarvon Mission first appeared: Betty Sewell , *Carnarvon: interaction of two cultures*, North Essendon: Vital Publications, 1990. Thank you to Churches of Christ in Australia for giving permission to reproduce those images here.

Lost mother

The land is my lost mother
I yearn to know and see
I slowly walk timidly into her arms
She caresses and nurtures me
Her beautiful fragrance and songs
Wash over me, giving me fresh dreams
Filling the emptiness, replacing my worth
Sadness and pain buried deep in the earth
She whispers and tells me that here I belong
Let your spirit be free, let your spirit be strong
This land is yours as far as the eyes can see
It flows in your blood right down to the sea
My spiritual totem she reveals to me
Emotions of peace, feelings of belonging
Her gentle soft tears drop from the sky
She is happy for she has found
Her precious lost child.

Preface

I lived my early years on a native mission in Western Australia — growing up without a mother's love. I was always searching for my people's language, dance, songs and stories. I went on to find some family, my culture, my identity and ultimately myself. In writing this book, I wanted to speak about what happened to us as a people, on a human level, through the eyes of a child.

There were many issues that I struggled with, unsure whether to reveal them in this book. Then I decided that these yarns should be told because, perhaps in some way, they may help other people who are struggling with a similar past.

My story is not about blame. It's about sharing history that belongs to all of Australia. I needed a push, but I am happy to finally give little Rhonda a voice, so that my words will live on after I leave this world. I want to thank each person who allowed me to use their name and photo, and, in those cases where the people are deceased, to the next of kin who gave their permission.

I realise that my memories of mission life and growing up as a naïve Aboriginal girl in 1950s and 1960s Australia will differ from many others. However, I hope that by hearing about my life, the wider community might become more aware and understand how the policies and experiences of the past impact the lives of our people today. I hope too that others like me will find the strength to talk about their lives, and get the help, comfort and healing they have missed all these years.

To my fellow Aboriginal readers, let us nurture our Indigenous spirit by holding on to our identity: be proud of who we are, what we have survived and where we come from. Remember, we are the first peoples of this land — Aboriginal land: always was, always will be. Remember the old ways of sharing and caring, our values, the true way. Remember to pass on language, stories and dances to keep our culture alive. Remember to respect our elders, our family and ourselves. Remember to stop and look back to know where we have been. Only then can we focus on moving forward.

Thank you for reading and for hearing my voice.

Aboriginal Blessings to you all.

– Aunty Rhonda Collard-Spratt, April 2017

Author's note

In 2012, I heard through the Murri grapevine that this Aboriginal art course was going to be run in our community. I was real excited. At that time, I was isolating myself and I felt it would be good to be in a space with other Aboriginal people. I was really looking forward to starting this program because I knew most of the Murri people in my area anyway.

The mentors for the program would be Aboriginal. I already knew Aunty Pat King — a highly respected elder, inspiring community leader and talented artist. And I'd heard of the renowned artist Aunty Sally Harrison.

On our first day, that's when I met Jacki who organised this art program. She'd worked with Aunty Pat at Ipswich City Council many years earlier. They'd had some great times, running dawn ceremonies at the old Purga Mission, west of Ipswich, and organising the first Sorry Day March through town. Jacki brought Aunty Pat and these other artists into our local community centre to share their skills and stories with us.

Before the art course, I had never set foot in that community centre. The first time I went, it was a bit scary. The energy there wasn't welcoming. The workers kept away from us. They all sat together by the door, chatting to each other, and staring at us. We knew it was a white space. But then, when I saw a few familiar faces of my friends, I felt at ease. To see Aunty Pat as well was great. With her there, I felt safe.

When I first saw Jacki, I thought, That's the hair I always wanted! Red hair. But then when she spoke, I just knew Jacki wasn't like those other women. I had a connection with her from that moment. For somebody to start a program just for us, they must have a good spirit, I thought.

We all felt comfortable with Jacki. Not many of us feel comfortable around white fellas, but Jacki never gave up on us. She fought for us.

The art program strengthened our connection to our communities, and we made spiritual connections. Jacki came over to see how we were going with our paintings. That way, she heard many of our stories, our personal stories that we were sharing with each other.

One day, not long into the program, I went into Jacki's office and sat with her and Aunty Pat for a while. I told them about the time when, aged about thirteen, I first met my mother, for just five minutes. I could tell Jacki was moved. It was like she got emu bumps all up her arms — that's what I call them. She turned to Aunty Pat who said, 'Someone should write this down. Jacki, you should write it.'

Jacki agreed that once she'd finished up with her job at that centre, she would contact me, and together we would write my life story.

The art program wasn't easy for Jacki, and it wasn't because of me or the other participants. For the first time, Jacki saw how unacceptable and cruel some people's attitudes and actions towards Aboriginal people can be. KEEP OUT signs went up, and locks were put on cupboards and doors. Jacki was told that us artists were not allowed to use the art supplies without a staff member unlocking the cupboard, and that we were not allowed to take our art home to work on. Jacki said that in over 20 years working in the community, she'd never faced such obvious discrimination. Soon participants in the program said they no longer wanted to turn up.

Then one day Jacki brought in Laurie Nilsen, a famous Aboriginal artist, and lecturer from Griffith University, to give us a talk. Jacki was hoping everyone would continue with the program. Sure enough, Laurie's talk worked its magic. In the end, though, the hurtful attitudes of workers at the centre became too much for Jacki to continue. But us participants saw it through. Jacki told me she was so proud when we put on a successful art exhibition and sold a lot of our work.

In February 2013, Jacki gave me a call and said she was excited to get started on putting together my memoir.

When I was fifty, I'd begun writing down memories from my life as a kid. So, when Jacki started working with me, I brought to her place all my thoughts and feelings on pieces of paper. I had no idea of how to write a story — I can speak it better than write it.

We started in her old house. Then in 2014, she moved. I love her new house. It's a big wooden home with a beautiful breeze. We call her office the story room. I love sitting in the comfy chairs and looking out at the trees, listening to the birds and the wind.

We always grabbed a cuppa before beginning work. Then we'd walk down to the story room and sit at the computer. First up, I'd start to remember a story. I spoke as Jacki typed down my words. Sometimes I emailed stuff through, but for me, I found it better to say it. Then Jacki put it in some kind of order. When things didn't sound right, we talked it through together until we were both happy. We laughed a lot, ate a lot, cried a lot, and somehow got some writing done. Maybe that's why it took such a long time to finish this book. Maybe we just enjoy each other's company.

Over this period, our friendship's gotten stronger, and we've become family. Jacki is my mob now and I'm part of her family.

Sadly, Aunty Patricia King passed away in early 2016. Jacki and me would both like to honour Aunty Pat by sharing my story with you.

1

A black girl in a white world

I was born in a black and white world. If you were white, everything was okay. You could do what you liked. But if you were black, your life was controlled by the government. We weren't seen as humans. We were treated as part of the flora and fauna. We weren't recognised as citizens in our own country until the Referendum in 1967.[1]

When I say they controlled our lives, I mean we had to live on the fringes of towns and on native missions and reserves. The missions were run either by the government or different churches. You couldn't marry who you fell in love with; you had to get permission from the government. You also had to get a permit to move from place to place. When you worked, they stole your wages. If you wanted to buy anything, you had to virtually beg for your money. You had to write a letter to the government to ask if you could buy a dress or shoes or stockings.[2]

I was born in Carnarvon, Western Australia, on 17 August 1951. I am Yamatji on my mother's side and Nyungar (some say 'Noongar') and Nhanda-Yamatji on my father's side. I am the first-born child of Alice Ethel Spratt, married name Webb, and Ronald Mack Ugle. They gave me the name Rhonda June Spratt. My maternal grandfather was Clarry Spratt and my grandmother was Edna Ronan.

I didn't grow up with my family because me and my baby sister, Debbie Anne Spratt, were taken from our mother and put into

Co/ Mrs Fleay
Gurrabilba Str.
Meekatharra
5 March 1950

Dear Mrs Stitfold,

Will you please send me a sunsuit a green one if possible. I'd like you to get me a pair of bathers and also a pair of wedgie sandals too, but if I haven't got enough money to get the sunsuit, and sandals, don't bother about them, but please get the bathers get sea green or blue, if you will please.

Thanking you very much

Sincerely yours

Alice Spratt

Mr. Lewis.

For advice, please, re Alice Spratt's trust account.

C. Stitfold
9/3/50

Letter from Alice Spratt to Mrs Stitfold, with annotation to Mr Lewis, 1950.[3]

Carnarvon Native Mission.[4] I was only three at the time and Debbie was just seven months old. I always knew that we had a mother somewhere; I just didn't know where she was.[5]

Unlike some other missions in Australia, at Carnarvon, no Aboriginal families lived together. It was just us kids and the white missionaries. Most mission people call their parents 'mother' and 'father'. We don't say 'mum' or 'dad' because we didn't know them.

The full name of our mission was Churches of Christ Carnarvon Native Mission. Me and Debbie grew up in dormitories — from the Kindergarten dormitory, to Junior Buds, to Junior Girls, to Senior Girls, to Teens Cottage, and finally to Home Girls. All this time, my sister and me were in different dormitories because we were different ages. We didn't get to play together. The only time we were in the same dormitory was my final year, when we were together in Teens Cottage.

On any day, we had to be up at 6 am and have our beds made with 'hospital corners'. As girls, we always had to wear aprons. I hate aprons today.

We all had different chores before breakfast. Some girls worked in the Kindergarten dormitory, others down at the big dining room kitchen. A huge table filled the centre of the dining room. Under it stood heavy trolleys of flour, sugar and salt, with lids to keep them from spoiling. We worked very hard. Working in the kitchen was the best because we stole a bit of food on the side — like some dried fruit from the pantry, which we hid in our aprons.

One of the jobs I hated was in the laundry, ironing. We couldn't go and play until we'd finished. We had to starch everything too. When I worked in the Junior Boys dormitory, it made me sad when the little boys wet their beds. They had to wash their sheets by hand as punishment, standing on a bucket at a big trough. They were too small and couldn't hang their sheets up, so I helped them.

The boys milked the cows, and worked in the vegetable gardens. They chopped enough wood to fill a big truck. Even us girls had to go out and fill that truck up with wood. We all sat high on the wood going home. It was hard work, but we liked going out in the bush.

The dining room was used for both meals and church. We had to polish that huge wooden floor too. Those electric polishers were enormous; they chucked us around. When the missionaries weren't looking, we had fun giving each other rides.

We prepared breakfast for them missionaries. I loved standing by Lynda James, one of the big girls, keeping warm and watching as she fried the eggs on the big wood stove, spooning the fat over the yolks as the bacon sizzled. It felt comforting being next to her, smelling the bacon and hearing it crackle. We had a whole chookyard, but we were never allowed to eat the eggs. The white missionaries ate them and sold the rest to the hospital or the towns people.

The missionaries sat at the head of the table in nice comfy chairs. We sat on stools. The missionaries always started off breakfast with grapefruit, which we segmented, sprinkled with brown sugar, and topped with a red cherry. Next, they enjoyed hot porridge, bacon, eggs, tomato on toast and a cup of tea. We, by contrast, ate porridge and bread with butter, Vegemite, or molasses — you know, like they feed horses.

One day, at breakfast in the big dining room, a missionary said grace. Then Miss Barton, the young missionary nurse who always smelt of antiseptic, announced, 'Now we'll say our own special little grace for our table.'

Each child was to say something. So, we bowed our heads and prayed. It was the turn of the boy next to me. His name was Marshall Kelly, but we nicknamed him Diamond Face because his face was that shape. We were always saying prayers for the Kellys. Some of Marshall's brothers and sisters got sent to Perth because they were sick a lot of the time.

Diamond Face began, 'Thank you Jesus for my ham and eggs.'

I elbowed him. 'Why are you thanking Jesus for ham and eggs? We never ever have ham and eggs, *they* do!'

'Rhonda Spratt! Open your ears!' Diamond Face shouted. 'I didn't thank Jesus for ham and eggs, I thanked him for my arms and legs!'

I got a scolding and a slap on the arm from Miss Barton. We all laughed about it later though.

We had three meals a day, but I was still hungry. That's why today, when I have a chop, there's nothing left of it — the bone is left clean. We even broke the bone and sucked out the marrow. I ate dried banana and orange skins off the ground too. On the odd occasion when we got an orange, I peeled off each segment, and ate just one little juicy droplet at a time to make the fruit last longer. When making dinner, I even ate the raw potatoes. After we'd had enough to eat, we weren't allowed to say we were full; we had to say, 'I've had elegant sufficiency', which means full anyway. I didn't say that very often.

We were, however, force-fed religion. We had Devotion before breakfast, Christian Endeavour during the week, and on Sunday we had morning church, Sunday school in the afternoon, then evening church. Occasionally, on a Sunday, we went to the native reserve. Their church was a bough shed — it had four posts with wire strung over the top, covered with branches and leaves.

The only thing good about Sundays was getting dressed in our church clothes. We wore pretty little dresses, and combed our hair back neatly, tied with colourful ribbons. We all had shiny shoes with white socks, and we each got a handkerchief. To keep myself from falling asleep, and to save my sanity, I made things out of my hanky. I could make roses, lollies and even a banana.

Growing up in the mission, we heard religious stories over and over for years. But I knew my people had our own beliefs. There was this knowing inside me. I resented the missionaries. During church services, they held up large posters of a big white cross over a straight and narrow road. Their pictures showed all of our people in the gutter.

The only enjoyable thing at church was the singing. Even today I can remember the words of all those songs. They are deeply etched into every fibre of my flesh.

One time, when I was about twelve, me and Debbie had to sing an item about Jesus. We were at the Christian Centre in Perth in front of a large congregation as we had come together with the Norseman Mission.[6] We began, 'More about Jesus would I know, more of His love to others show ...' I can't remember who sang a wrong word, but there we were, standing on stage in front of all those people, laughing and giggling our heads off. Luckily, because so many people were around, we weren't punished, we just got told off.

Only one missionary man could play the piano well, honky tonk style. Honky Tonk wore his pants at high tide, up around his armpits. He was always playing friendly, putting his arm around you and smiling at you. Years later, we found out he was a paedophile. He was messing with the boys, not the girls. People want to deny that this happened, but it did. When we were in the Senior Girls dormitory, this man would come in when we were showering. When we turned away from him, he would shout, 'Turn around and face me and scrub your crotch!'

One time, one of the mission boys, Laurie Tittum, overheard some missionaries talking about the Senior Girls being 'full of virgins'. He got worried and came over to our yard and told us. He wasn't supposed to be there. Soon after, we could hear Laurie screaming, getting a flogging in the Superintendent's office. Laurie was always looking out for us. He was good at killing rats in the barn with a ging too, so we nicknamed him Rat. Rat was a clever detective — he saw things the rest of us missed.

We were told that Jesus loved us, but no one ever cuddled us. No one ever comforted us. No one ever said, 'You're a good kid, Rhonda.' I grew up feeling alone — a black girl in a white world.

They taught me well. I could speak their language. I wore their clothes. I read their Bible. I sang their hymns. But in my heart, I resented them for trying to make me white. It was like being dropped head first into a tin of white paint. But the real me was still there — they couldn't wash away 60,000 years of Dreaming and history that tie me forever to this sacred land: the river, the sky, the claypans, the sandhills, the wildflowers and the sea — that is me.

Being apart from my family and any kind of affection had a big effect on me, even at the time. Once, in the middle of the night, when I was about thirteen, I woke up. The night was completely dark and still. No trees rustled. I sat straight up in bed listening, just listening. But all was silent. Maybe God had come back and taken everyone away, leaving only me. I thought that all the mission kids and adults had gone and left me here all alone. Even God didn't want me. It was such a lonely feeling. All my life I'd heard about God as love. But I didn't feel loved at all. I just laid back and cried.

The one time of the week that we loved was Saturday afternoon when we were allowed to go for walks. We called it 'the bush', but we had to ask politely, 'Can we go for a walk into "the common"?', a very English term. Usually there was a group of about four or five of us, including Beverley Pickett, Roslyn Flanagan, Irene Tittum and sometimes little Marjorie Hughes who, when she was nervous, used to stutter back then.

The next property was owned by a white man named Tucker Reynolds. Beverley would ask the girls to hold the barbed wire open and I'd climb through, coming face-to-face with a big bullock. I'd stamp my foot at him, and he'd stamp back, kicking up the dust. Soon he'd put his head down, ready to charge at me. But when he charged, I'd run at the opening and dive back through the fence, hitting the dirt on the other side, with the other girls shouting and laughing.

My favourite time in the common was spring. The land was fragrant with flowers and full of bush tucker like blackberries, orange berries (we called them wild orange), wild pear or gogola, and yams. Carnarvon is semi-desert, so when it rains a bit everything blooms. My favourites included everlastings (white people call them paper daisies) in pink, yellow and white; button flowers, yellow like the sun;

fluffy pussycat tails in a beautiful soft mauve colour; and purple vetch — that's what we called it — in the shape of a heart. I always felt free going out there, not having to worry about chores. We grabbed sticks and drew hopscotch squares in the sand. We played it in a circle, starting from the outside in, like a snail shell.

Springtime, or after rain, was good eating for other things too. Us girls followed the tracks of little insects that lived beneath the surface of the earth and left mounds. 'Iddy-iddy' we called them. We dug them up for fish bait. We could see all of the animal tracks then too. We got pieces of wire and bent them like fishing rods to catch big grubs as long as your hand from around the roots of gum trees. We fished them out and cooked them up for a snack. Someone told me later that they grow into these great moths. Then I felt sorry for them, because we ate them.

I often walked alone to the little creek near us and sat up high on a branch of my favourite gum tree, watching the birds flying above, and the big bullfrog tadpoles swimming in the clear water below. I sat there for hours, watching sunlight dance on the water, wondering what my life would be, thinking that I hated the past, but was scared of the future. Being still for that moment, surrounded by nature and without any other kids around me, was good for my soul and good for my spirit.

Being a part of the natural world gave me a lot of joy. Here I could be at one with nature, the creek, the birds, the animals and the bugs. I spent time with nature and talked to her as if she were my mother.

By the water grew little royal-blue flowers with a yellow centre. They looked beautiful against the red earth. I would sit, taking all this in, looking at the reeds and freshwater turtles in the creek that was cool and peaceful and just for me. I didn't ever want to leave it and be back in the dormitories, in the noise, among the people.

Gifts from nature

I drink the dew drops from the wildflowers
That grow on this sacred ancient red land,
So cool and so fresh to the touch on my tongue
Taste the sweet nectar, fragrance fill my soul

I see trees, half-human, standing tall and strong
Stretch their limbs up high into the daytime sky
Seeking warmth and life-giving light
From the sun god that lives so far away

I hear the wind sing her gentle lullaby
As she hugs and caresses our mother the earth,
The voice of the magpies, so beautiful,
Soaks into my heart with love, peace and joy

Find golden gumdrops on acacia trees
Juicy orange and blackberries wait, just for me,
Take only what you need, there's no need for greed
The gifts from nature are here for you and me.

Granny Ruby Beasley came into my life when she started work in the mission laundry. One day she just came up and told me that she was my Grandfather Clarrie's sister. Her maiden name was Spratt, just like me and Debbie. She told us who all her sisters and brothers were. She'd grown up on Moore River Native Settlement made famous by the film *Rabbit-Proof Fence*.[7,8] Through Granny Ruby we got to know who our family were, but by name only.

Granny Ruby lived with many other Aboriginal families on the Gascoyne riverbank in a tin humpy. Me and Debbie visited her at the camp when we were allowed to go for our Saturday afternoon walks. Every time we went there, Granny was drinking. She would tell me and Debbie not to drink, and then ask us to sing Christian songs. We began, 'What a friend we have in Jesus, all our sins and griefs to bear. What a privilege to carry everything to God in prayer...'

She would start to cry. By this time, me and Debbie were crying too, but still singing, sitting on the red ground. Before we left to return to the mission, Granny would give me a matchbox full of silver coins. She told me to share it with my little sister, which I always did.

I'll never forget Granny Ruby. She was the first person to show me and Debbie true love. She was family. Our blood was the same.

One very hot day, all us mission kids were swimming at the netting crossing. I was having fun until a big girl started laughing at my Granny. She could see Granny Ruby in the distance, carrying her jimmy-john or plonk. Then all the kids started laughing at her as she fell over in the dry riverbed.

This made me so wild. I started shouting at everybody, but they still kept carrying on. I tucked my dress in my pants, fixing to fight the lot of them. I was angry that they were making fun of my precious Gran. I started yelling at them to fight me. In the mission, you had to fight to survive. But nobody stepped up. They knew I was a good fighter.

When no one took up my challenge, I ran down the dry riverbed and pulled Granny Ruby to her feet. After picking up her bottles of drink, I helped her back to the humpy. When we got there, she asked me to pour the drink into another container because her hands were too shaky.

As I did this for her she cried, 'Look at your hands! They're so steady!'

She placed her long brown fingers on my shoulder, looked me in the eyes, and said, 'Don't you ever start drinking like me.'

So, on that hot day, in the middle of that sandy riverbed, I made a promise to myself that I would never let alcohol be my boss. Granny Ruby's words of wisdom are still part of my life today. She gave me identity. She gave me history. She gave me family. And she gave me love that I had never known.

The river

The river that I love is mostly dry
Tall gum trees watch over her
Swaying gently to the warm summer breeze
I walk along the riverbed looking for pretty stones
I am alone
I hear the sound of crunching sand beneath my Yamatji feet
I am alone

I stop and stare into the shallow water puddles
Reflections of the sky
Reflections of me
I reach into the water
and touch the clouds and then the sun
I am alone

I listen to the humming of the wind
Singing her song to the land and me
I watch the ants scurrying along
I am alone

I smell the scent of rain
I hear the whispers of a storm
I hold my riverstones tight in my Yamatji hands
I am alone

I gaze into the dark sky and tremble at the thought of lightning
Dragonflies with beautiful wings and bulging eyes
dart and dance silently over still fresh water
I am alone

Raindrops shatter the stillness of the water like a breaking mirror
I watch the circles of water rush to greet each other like old friends

I know the music of the storm
I know the songs of the rain
I know the stories of the river
I know the dance of the land
I am not alone
The river that I love is mostly dry.

One time when we were little, visiting Granny Ruby down by the river, her son was there. He strummed a guitar and sang 'Showers of Blessing'. Later, he came to the mission evening church and sang. So, it was Uncle Jim Beasley who inspired me to learn to play guitar.

A big-name country singer, Buddy Williams, once visited the mission too. Later, I learnt that Buddy was a 'forgotten Australian'. He'd been brought out from England during the Second World War as a child, without his parents. I often wondered why he'd visited us. Maybe it was because he understood what it was like to grow up without the love of a mother or father.

Buddy stayed and had tea with us in the dining room. His group sat on the stage above and, after our meal, they entertained us. I still remember a special song Buddy sang to us all those years ago. It's called 'There's a little red bonnett our baby wore'. He told us the story about the song and how he lost his baby girl who was killed in a train accident as they were crossing a railway line. I felt really honoured to have this famous singer visit, talk with us, and give us his precious time.

As the sun went down, the band had to leave. They travelled down the dirt track with all us mission kids running after their car, waving as they left us in a cloud of dust. That fond memory has lived with me all this time.

2

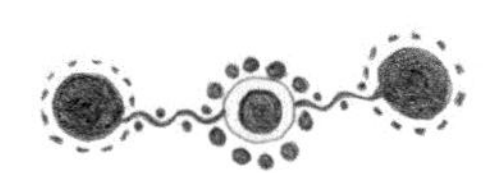

Childhood games and mission ways

In the early years, we went to the mission school. This school had two rooms, two teachers, and all the children from Grades One to Six. I can't remember learning much, but we did fun things like basketweaving, painting, picking wildflowers, and playing in the bush. I especially remember getting honey from the bees.

One of the boys — usually Peter Coppin, he was Ngarluma-Yindjibarndi from up Roebourne way — would climb a tall gum tree with a stick in his hand to stir the bees up. Peter moved like a warrior, with purpose. Soon angry bees would be flying everywhere. Us kids on the ground wore hessian bags on our heads like cloaks, and waved wattle branches in our hands, ready to shoo the bees away.

We never got much honey, but we had lots of fun trying. I never ever got stung, but Bunda did. Right between her eyes on her nose. Her face swelled up and she had two big, shiny, bung eyes.

Lots of kids got bung eyes from flies biting them too. When this happened, we picked up warm stones from the ground and placed them on our sores, the way the older kids at the mission had showed us.

Once a month the missionaries held a birthday party to celebrate every child born in that month. All the birthday kids sat at one special table with a birthday cake. We each got finger food and a little basket of lollies. The oldest child at the birthday table lit the candles, and the youngest had the honour of blowing them out. I never got to blow out the candles, but I lit them once, when I was sixteen.

After the party, we watched films. The films were usually about cowboys, suitable for children, and we always ended with a Christian film. One memorable film was *Shadow of the Boomerang*, a movie made in 1960 starring Jimmy Little. As a young Aboriginal kid, it was exciting seeing someone of your own race up there on the big screen, singing. It made me proud that one of our mob was performing, and I never forgot it because music is my passion, and Jimmy Little is one of my heroes.

When I was in the room for Grades One to Three, our teacher was Miss Maclinton. She was Scottish with real fair skin and fine blonde hair, which was permed. Because it stood right out, just like fairy floss, the flies got caught in the ends of her frizz. One time, Marine James brought these spiky doublegees into class. She put them on Miss Maclinton's chair. When the teacher sat down, her face turned bright red, and she quickly jumped up.

'Who put the doublegees on my chair?'

She stood there, rubbing her behind. We'd all lost our tongues. We stared at her, wide-eyed and silent. When she turned her back, we chuckled under our breath.

Miss Maclinton taught us many Scottish songs. She sang, 'You take the high road, and I'll take the low road...', and 'I am a soldier, a Scottish soldier who wandered far away...', and the one called 'Bonnie Charlie'. She would get us to repeat the words of the song exactly like her. Because she was a Scotswoman with a very strong accent, when she taught us these songs, we too sang with strong Scottish accents. It must have sounded strange, these Scottish voices coming from the mouths of little Aboriginal kids.

The boys had their yard, and us girls had ours. We were kept apart — boys and girls always separated. In the mission yard, us girls played many different games. We were never allowed to play inside, only if it rained, and that was very rare. We didn't have any toys, but we had a swing set and monkey bars. Mostly, though, we made up games with things we found laying around.

Me and my friends loved making mud pies. We decorated them with wildflowers, sticks and stones. One time, the Senior Girls tried to make us Junior Girls eat the mud pies. Marjorie and Roslyn and some others ate them, but I took off, running flat out, and they couldn't catch me. Those girls who ate the pies got the goon-nas. They made me proper sorry. Poor fullas!

Other games we played was rounders, and skittles with empty tins stacked up with stones and broken bits of asbestos. We also played this game 'Stacks on the mill, more on still' where one person lies down and each girl piles up on her, and another on top and then another until the girl on the bottom can't stand it, and we'd all fall over.

We played skipping with one big rope too. I was good at this. It was hard for them to get me out, even skipping pepper, skipping flat out. Another game was 'Guess who?' where one girl turns away and shuts her eyes, and the rest hide under a big cloth. Just by feel, the girl has to guess who is under the sheet. We invented these games to help fill the time and bring a bit of fun into our lives. Maybe that's why we became so creative.

One day, me and the girls were drawing on the dormitory walls with charcoal. First, we drew pictures. Then, Roslyn Flanagan came up with the idea to write about the two single missionary ladies.

'Miss Barton fell down fartin', we wrote, and all busted out laughing. Then we wrote, 'Miss Maclinton got up stinkin'.

We were having a great time creating all this graffiti until a missionary we nicknamed Ghost Who Walks appeared. He came up and jarred us all. He told us we better get all this writing off the walls quick smart, and we better use plenty of 'elbow grease'.

We all huddled together.

'Okay,' Lynda James began. 'Who's going inside to ask for the elbow grease?'

Marjorie bravely raised her hand. Head down and biting her lip, Marjorie entered the clothing room.

'Um…exc-use me, Sssir. C-can we have a j-jar of elbow g-grease p-please?'

'It doesn't come in a jar!' the missionary yelled. 'It means you have to use your energy real hard!'

We were all waiting outside for Marjorie and the jar of elbow grease. When she came out and told us what it was, we had a good old laugh. We got those dormitory walls clean by using water and our 'elbow grease'.

Climbing the tamarix trees was another favourite game of mine. I sucked their long, thin, salty leaves and admired their soft, pink flowers, which were long and thin too with a sweet honey smell that the bees just loved.

After rain, these trees held on to the water. Sunlight danced and reflected through the raindrops that hung loosely on their delicate leaves, catching me in a trance. The droplets sparkled like diamonds with all the colours of the rainbow. For a time, I was lost to this special moment of beauty, and all the world was blocked out by my daydream. Soon enough I snapped back to the mission yard again, with the noise of the girls filling my ears.

I called out to my friends. 'Hey, Beverley Pickett Anna Hayes! Marjorie Hughes! Come here! I wanna show you fullas something!'

You can tell us Carnarvon mob because we always call each other by our full names.

They rushed over to me under the tree to see the pretty raindrops. While they stared up, I jumped up high, grabbed a branch, and shook it so hard that the rain fell all over us.

'Baalay!' they laughed, flicking raindrops from their hair.

I like rain. As a kid, I watched raindrops fall into puddles of water. Droplets hit the water then bounced up into tear-shapes in the air then fell back, melting into the muddy pools. Ripple by ripple, the droplets spread to the puddle's edge, keeping me lost in my dream world.

The powerful smell of rain on earth is my favourite scent — so fresh, so earthy, so potent. It is the essence and pure fragrance of Mother Earth, grounding and focusing me to the spirit of this ancient land.

There were days I sat by myself on the grass near the dripping tap, watching the dragonflies hover then dart in for a drink. Chasing them, trying to catch one, was no good because they were too clever to get caught.

One day, I found a dead dragonfly laying on the ground. Picking it up gently, I stared at it thinking it was the most beautiful thing I'd ever seen, so pretty and dainty — a body light and very skinny. Its eyes were like big chunks of crystal glass, round, smooth and clear, and its wings were fine and thin. Dragonflies' eyes and wings fascinated me, and I wanted to be like them. I had always wanted big eyes, and the girls and me used to say that our shoulder bones would grow wings when we became angels.

Dragonfly

With delicate wings you glide through the air
I sit and watch you with wonder and awe
Can I join you? Be just like you?
Share with me your secrets and your lore
You fly so free for all the world to see
Soft beautiful see-through wings
That catch all the colours of the rainbow
Reflecting in harmony from your heart
With big eyes so green so pretty so bold
You see the world and the visions she holds

Oh I wish, oh how I wish
I had eyes just like you
Green with sparkles of gold and specks of blue
And oh so big, yes eyes so big
Yes I wish I wish I was you
To be beautiful to be free
Oh dragonfly maybe I should be happy
Just being plain old Rhonda, me.

We had loads of fun with old hessian bags too. We built cubby houses from them, made hats from them, and undid the strands to give us long hair that we wore with style in the yard. We plaited this hair, wore ponytails, or just let it hang long.

'Byay!' Beverley Pickett would shout, parading around. 'Look at my long hair! When I grow up, this is how my hair will look.'

We walked around feeling real pretty with our bag hair on, flicking it this way and that, thinking we were movie stars, like Patsy-Ann Noble. She was very beautiful with her long, jet-black hair.

None of us liked getting our hair cut. They cut it so short we called it the 'chooky neck' haircut. I wanted to grow my hair long.

One time, they were calling in each girl to get their hair cut. When it was my turn, I ran and hid, crawling far under the Junior Girls dormitory. They called and called for me. No one found me for hours. When it started getting dark, I got frightened for ngoojidees, so I crawled out of my hiding space. The missionaries immediately grabbed me and gave me an ugly chooky neck haircut. I wanted to cry, but I never let anyone see me cry.

My sister Debbie and me both had straight hair and small eyes. Wishing that my hair was curly and my eyes were big became a major pastime. Kids who looked like that were admired by both the missionaries and the tourists. And the tourists gave them lollies. So, when the tourist buses came, I ran into the dormitory and hid under my bed, even though I wished for a lolly.

At night in bed when the lights were out, I twisted strands of my hair and slid in bobby pins to hold it in place. In the morning before anyone was up, I took out the bobby pins.

'Byay!' I shouted to all the girls. 'Look at my hair! It's getting curly!'

Nobody cared.

Under the cover of darkness, I stretched my eyes wide, over and over again, wishing they would grow big. But this never worked either. I wanted to be admired, to be liked, to be given lollies.

Beverley Pickett had the hair I wanted. It was blondish, curly, and very fine. But Beverley hated her hair. She was always washing it, and trying to comb it straight. Tourists loved Beverley. One time when we went to Perth for holidays, when we were about thirteen, a white family invited Beverley and me to their place for Sunday dinner. All the kids without contact with their families were taken to Perth for holidays. After the morning church service, we would line up and white families would choose Aboriginal kids to take home for the day. They had really only wanted Beverley, because of her hair. That white family were still admiring it as we prepared dinner at their house that night. They just ignored me. I got wild, picked up the potatoes, and started chucking them at everyone.

When she was in Junior Girls and I was in Senior Girls, Debbie and me shared the yard. But, because of the age difference, we played separately in our own groups. One day, I was alone on a swing. My little sister came and sat on the other swing. We didn't speak for quite a while. We were both just swinging, backwards and forwards in silence. It was good just being in this space with only me and Debbie.

Finally, Debbie turned to me. 'I'm proud of you, Rhonda.'

I didn't know what to say. We just started to giggle and giggle, swinging higher and higher, giggling our heads off. Up until then, no one in my life had paid me any kind words. And here was my pretty little baby sister, Debbie Spratt, speaking from her heart. You see, during that week, we'd had our sports day. I won all my races and became the schoolgirl champion. That was why Debbie was proud of me. This beautiful memory and her loving words will stay with me now and forever. She is my heart.

Later that same day, before sundown, me and another girl got into a fight. She took off running into the dormitory to dob on me to the missionaries for hitting her. But she'd hit me, and I'd hit her. It was hit for hit. I forgot she went to dob on me.

In the meantime, me and Beverley Pickett was playing. I was laying under the swing while Beverley was swinging, standing up above me. *Whoossh! Whoossh*! She came close to the ground where I lay. The blue sky and the wind of Beverley passed over me. We were going to take it in turns, laying under the swing.

Next thing, a big fat missionary, the cook we nicknamed Balloon Bum, called my name. 'Rhonda Spratt! Come into the clothing room at once!' She sounded wild.

Without thinking, I quickly sat up straight. With its full force, and with Beverley on it, the swing hit me hard, fair in the back of the head. Stars floated in my eyes, and I felt dizzy. I reached back and felt warm blood trickling through my short black hair.

My wobbly legs slowly steadied, and I tried to shake out the stars. Somehow I made it into the clothing room. Balloon Bum kept me waiting a while because she was calling in the girls from the different dormitories for their night showers.

While I waited, I looked around the clothing room. A big table with a sewing machine rested up against the wall under a row of louvres. They used this table to check our heads for nits and headlice. They'd spread out a white sheet and use a nit comb. The lice fell on the sheet, so you could easily see them. Then we cracked them between our fingers. I liked the popping sound of nits and headlice. But if you had lice, they put kerosene on your head and rubbed it all through your hair. It wasn't nice and it smelt ugly.

A side cupboard leaned up against one wall. On top of it, at eye level, stood religious pictures, very colourful and bright. High in the top cupboard that reached the ceiling, I knew they had locked away my green tea set. They only let me play with it in this room by myself from time to time. I loved that little green tea set. I wanted to climb up on a stool, find it, and keep it with me for always. Why did they keep it locked up and away from me? Over the years, I have wondered who would have sent me this tea set. Could it have been from Mother? I discovered a long time later that green was her favourite colour.

Finally, footsteps. I knew it was her because it was footsteps with shoes on, and us kids didn't wear shoes. Then she was in the room with me. Balloon Bum had short hair parted on the side, and always wore dresses that were higher at the back because of her massive behind.

I didn't tell Balloon Bum that I was hurt and felt sick from the hit to my head.

'Tell me why you were fighting!' Her big round face puffed up like it might pop.

I couldn't speak. I wanted to tell her that I was just sticking up for myself, but instead I stood there quiet, head down, looking at my feet.

It seemed like forever, her waiting for me to talk, to tell her what happened. I wanted to, but couldn't. Her white voice broke the silence.

'Hold your hands out!'

The cane cracked down hard on both my hands. Her yellow teeth gave a half-smile. My sore, dizzy head was now matched by two sore hands as well. I wanted to cry, but I held back the tears. I wasn't going to show her my pain.

'Go and have a shower, and put your pyjamas on!'

All the other girls were showered and already in bed, listening to a Bible story, so the whole bathroom was mine. After running naked down the long passageway, I stood under the warm water, washing away my blood, my silent tears, and my sadness. The warm water comforted me. That was all the comfort I had. I dried my aching little body, put on my summer pyjamas, and walked to our room.

Next minute, Balloon Bum stormed back in.

'Rhonda Spratt! Take your pyjamas off, and come to the clothing room at once!'

Back in the clothing room, that sick yellow smile reappeared.

'Put your hands out! This is hurting me more than it hurts you,' she said strangely. She had checked the soap and it was dry, so she caned me again for not using the soap. 'Go to the bathroom, and this time make sure you use the soap!'

With rage and hurt in my heart, I turned to look at their precious Christian images staring back at me from the top of the cupboard. The missionaries said that God was love. But what was love? Where was love? I didn't know what love was. No mummy or daddy kissed me goodnight. No one cared when I got hurt or lost my baby teeth.

With all these feelings of being unloved and being a nobody's child spinning in my sore head, I moved to the side cupboard. I raised my bony kid arm, and, with one mighty swing, I smashed every one of those colourful religious pictures of Baby Jesus, Mary, and the donkey. They fell in slow motion. Breaking glass hit the hard, shiny floorboards. Their many pieces now lay broken, silent and still.

As I raced out of the clothing room and back to the lonely bathroom, Balloon Bum's booming voice followed me.

'Rhonda Spratt! Get back here at once!'

Not wanting to be flogged again, I ignored her. Back under the shower, I stood there slowly using the soap, softly sobbing so no one could hear.

'Mummy, Daddy! Mummy, Daddy! I want my Mummy, Daddy!' my monotone voice called to the warm water.

Pyjamas on, I walked, aching, to our room. No one spoke to me. Silently, I climbed into bed and tucked the sheet and blankets around my head and body, like a cocoon. I have always felt safe like this. My silent rocking back and forth finally brought sleep, and took away my pain and misery.

It's healed now, but I still carry the scar on my head from that day when the swing hit me. It's a smooth scar where no hair can grow.

Boys and girls were always kept apart. The boys had their dormitories and yards where they lived and played, and us girls had ours. When they took us on picnics, the girls travelled on the bus, and the boys on the truck. In church, the boys sat on the left, and us girls on the right. The only times we were together were in class, on the school bus, and at meal times in the big dining room.

As a Junior Girl, I didn't like boys or boy germs. If anyone teased me about a boy, or told me that he liked me, I screamed at them to shut up. Then I waited until we were at school, ran up to that boy and punched him on the arm. 'I don't like you, so there!'

I'd fling my nose up in the air and walk off in a huff. Sometimes, silence was better. I just rushed up to them with a wild look and hit them. This was my way of sorting things out.

As a kid, I felt all alone in this world with no family to give me guidance or emotional support. All I had were my mission sisters and brothers, but we couldn't help each other because we were all in the same boat, with no paddle or life jackets. You either swam or you sank. Not wanting to drown, I swam. Not trusting the missionaries, I never talked to them about anything. They made me feel like I was a pest or nuisance. So I took it all on my little kid shoulders, and did the best I could.

As time went on, I started to like this one mission boy, Ted. Ted had dark hair and fair skin. He smelt of Velvet soap, and was tall with kissable lips. There was no punching Ted on the arm, or saying I didn't like him, because I did like him. And I knew he liked me too.

At first, I ignored him. Then he started teasing me and twisting my arm. Finally, we became girlfriend and boyfriend, but only from a distance. We gave each other shy looks and smiles. We were about eleven years old.

On Saturdays, some parents took their kids out of the mission for the day. I would stand by the mission fence alone watching them as they walked down the road together holding hands with their loved ones, their family. I wished and prayed hard that someone would come for me and Debbie. But no one ever came for us.

One Saturday, Ted's family came and took him and his brothers and sisters out. When he came back, he gave me a Cherry Ripe chocolate bar. It was the first chocolate I had ever tasted, and it was delicious. It tasted of coconut, cherries, and chocolate — heaven in my mouth. I took small bites to make it last longer. I didn't want it to end.

One day, when I was about ten years old, a letter arrived for me from my mother. I had never received a letter in my life. I started running around the dining room, waving it above my head.

'Hey! Byay! Look you fullas, I got a letter!'

'Well open it and read it,' Irene Tittum, Laurie's aunty (Laurie's 'mum' in the blackfella way; Laurie's father's youngest sister) cried.

So, sitting on the cold, shiny floor that I had polished many times, I read my first letter. A letter from Mother. Like all of our mail, the envelope was already opened, and the letter read by the missionaries.

Inside was a letter, a Christmas card, and a pound note. The letter asked me to share the money with my little sister, Debbie. I knew that the envelope would get lost, so I memorised the address. It was lasered into my memory forever:

Mrs A. E. Webb,
c/– Gogo Station via Fitzroy Crossing
West Kimberley WA[1]

From that day on, I started writing to Mother. I wrote every week. Sometimes, I even made Debbie write too. I gave the letters to one of the missionaries to post. I wrote these letters from the age of ten until I was sixteen. I never got one reply.

3

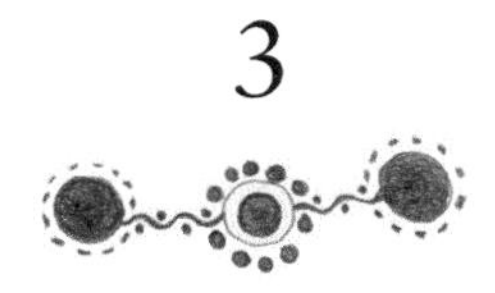

The birds and the bees

In 1962, a couple of years after the assimilation laws came in, the mission school closed and we were bussed into the town school or white school.[1] What a culture shock! I was in Grade Five and about ten years old.

We had our own Aboriginal 'mission talk', and the other kids couldn't understand us. The teachers at town school told us our language was 'rubbish'. At the mission, we nicknamed one missionary Scrubbo because he washed our mouths out with soap as punishment for using our languages. Our mission talk came from the kids who still had contact with their families. Some of them didn't come under the Native Act because they didn't fit the criteria, so they went out for weekends to see their families.[2] Many years later, I sent away to the different language centres in Western Australia for recordings of Aboriginal languages. The one in Geraldton sent me a tape. I wept. I said to myself, 'This is real language, not rubbish.'

Straight across from town school was the native hospital. Aboriginal people wrapped in bandages and dressed in white pyjamas sat on the veranda in the cool. I can only wonder at the differing conditions between the native hospital and the mainstream hospital.

When we came to the town school, I knew we hadn't had much education, so I put my head down and tried my hardest. I never ever came first in the town school, but I did get a second and a third out of all the class, both black and white.

DEPARTMENT OF NATIVE WELFARE — Form DNW 6C

REPORT ON INMATE — 3138

Carnarvon MISSION

Report to be completed and forwarded to the nearest Field Office by 31st December of year concerned.

GENERAL PROGRESS REPORT FOR YEAR ENDED 64

NAME OF CHILD Rhonda Spratt DATE OF BIRTH 17.8.51

ADMITTED 12.12.54

FATHER

MOTHER

PARENTS' ADDRESS

SCHOOL ATTENDING Carnarvon GRADE

GENERAL COMMENT BY SCHOOL TEACHER FROM SCHOOL REPORT ON ABILITY AND PROGRESS Satisfactory

COMMENT ON TRADE TRAINING (IF APPLICABLE)

MEDICAL AND DENTAL O.K.

CONDUCT O.K.

*REMARKS BY MISSION SUPERINTENDENT

DATE 29-12-64

MISSION SUPERINTENDENT

COMMENT BY DISTRICT OFFICER TO DIVISIONAL SUPT: North West

Satisfactory

DATE 13.1.65 DISTRICT OFFICER

COMMISSIONER OF NATIVE WELFARE:
(Comments by Divisional Supt.)

DATE 3.2.65 DIVISIONAL SUPT.

This document was released under the Freedom of Information Act 1992 by the Department for Child Protection

*In your Report please indicate whether child is expected to return for further education or is

'Report on Inmate', dated 29 December 1964. This is the only school report made available to Rhonda of her entire school life. The names and address of her parents were either not filled in at the time or were deleted by Freedom of Information, as are any detailed comments by, or signatures of, authorities involved. As provided by FOI, Department of Child Protection, WA, decision date: 27 March 2013.

Around this time, I also became involved in the Brownies and Girl Guides. We had a separate Girl Guides to the white kids, even when we started white school in town.

In 1963, Queen Elizabeth toured Australia for the fiftieth anniversary of the naming of Australia's capital, Canberra. Some of us Aboriginal girls, including Roslyn Flanagan and me, were chosen to see her. We travelled from Carnarvon to Geraldton in the back of a truck, yarning and laughing all the way.

When we arrived, the missionaries billeted us out separately to white families. The family I stayed with lived on a sandhill near a big water tank. That day, we had to polish our shoes and badges. At the wharf, we formed a guard of honour and saluted Her Majesty as she rode past. The Queen looked our way and smiled at me and Roslyn.

The next day, Sunday, was Mother's Day. I had never heard of Mother's Day before. The family and me walked to a beautiful church. It felt huge. During the service, the priest called every child up to receive a red rose to give to their mother for Mother's Day. Each one walked up, but I stayed sitting in my pew.

When every child had received their rose, they realised I didn't have one. So, they called me up the front with everyone now seated, watching as I received a rose from the preacher. A rose for Mother. I had no mother to give it to. I watched all the other children give their roses to their mothers.

After the service, we walked back up the sandhill along a dirt track. The family walked ahead, with me lagging behind, looking at the rose and smelling it, feeling sad. For all I knew, my mother was dead. I turned around to face where we'd come from, and slung the red rose onto the dirt track.

Town school was over for the day. When the school bus arrived, we always sat in the same seats. Mine was in the second last row, back left. Marjorie Hughes and me shared this spot.

On our trip back to the mission, Marjorie showed me this book about Australian wildlife she got from the library. When we looked at books together, we each picked one side of the book. Everything on your side belonged to you, and everything on the other side belonged to the other person.

Here we were boasting, 'Hey! Look what I've got!'

There were lovely pictures of kangaroos, emus, and all the cuddly bush animals. Then Marjorie turned the page. What a fright!

I screamed, chucked the book, and jumped up high, hitting my head on the racks where we put our school bags. There, staring back at me in full colour and looking so real, was a picture of a snake. I told Marjorie that I didn't want to look at the book anymore. We both had a good laugh, and me a sore head.

In the past, snakes didn't scare me. We even went looking for them under logs and old tins. But this all changed one day when Peter Coppin caught a coppertail on the flat. Peter picked it up, and swung it about wildly as he chased us girls with it. As a champion runner back in them days, I didn't think he could get me. I was running flat out with Peter right behind me, swinging this scaly milyura. And guess what? I tripped on some stones, and fell flat on my tummy.

That's when Peter put the snake down my back. It was thrashing and whipping about. It got caught on my apron strings, so it couldn't fall through to the ground. I got back on my feet and screamed all the way to the dormitory, trying to rip the apron off. Eventually, the snake fell to the ground. To this very day, I'm afraid of snakes.

When I turned twelve, they moved me from Junior Girls to the Senior Girls dormitory. Here I felt safe with the big girls. We even had a little drawer on the wall above our beds to keep our treasures in. In there, I kept my one purple hair roller and my Bible — all I had to my name. I don't remember who gave the hair roller to me. The missionaries gave us Bibles. The only things I liked in that book were my pressed wildflowers.

One evening, they called us Senior Girls into the common room. The common room had a big wooden table, a beautiful big black piano to play 'Chopsticks' on, and a blackboard. We sat on the cold floor in front of the blackboard.

Honky Tonk stood before us with his hands on his hips. He announced that he was going to tell us about 'the birds and the bees'. I thought he was going to teach us that song that goes, 'Let me tell you about the birds and the bees and the flowers and the trees and the moon up above...', but that wasn't it. He was trying to tell us about the facts of life, about sex.

The missionary drew on the blackboard one frog sitting on top of another frog. What did he mean? I thought he meant that we shouldn't play leapfrog anymore because we could get pregnant. We all left the common room more confused than ever.

Recently, some of the mission brothers told me about the sex talk the boys had in their common room with the missionary lady. During the discussion, a boy raised his hand.

'Please Miss, can you tell me how many bones and joints I have in my penis?'

The lady replied, 'You have no bones or joints there. It's just a muscle, dear. It's just a muscle.'

We can look back at this now and have a good laugh, but at the time it wasn't funny. Just one hour to teach us about the facts of life. All those years in their care, and only once did they ever talk to us about this, yet they spent countless hours and years teaching us about their religion, over and over again. They wanted to save our souls; that's what I believe. They fed us, they clothed us, they housed us, and they Christianised us, but they didn't care about our emotional wellbeing. We were left to deal with these issues by ourselves.

Looking back, I can see some good times together with lots of sadness. The good times for me were picnics at Shelly Beach — now called New Beach — Miaboolya Beach, One Tree Point, the Blow Holes, the river, and my favourite place, Rocky Pool. To go to Rocky Pool, all the girls travelled on the bus, and the boys in the mission truck.

Rocky Pool is special. It's part of the Gascoyne River, the longest river in Western Australia. We called it the 'upside down river' because the water soaks in, leaving golden sand on top, and water running under it. The river looks dry, but there's always water there. Beautiful river gums line the bank, which is ochre red rock. Maybe that's how Rocky Pool got its name. Here I had fun looking for pretty river stones. I spent hours alone doing this, and swimming in the fresh cool water, feeling the hot sun on my dark skin, and the softness of the river sand beneath my feet. I will never forget this place. The last time I was there I was about fourteen years old.

Happy times for us kids were like when we was taken to see the river coming down. This happened when it rained inland where the river is born. We would race to meet the red-brown water as it crawled slowly, ankle-deep to the sea. But we had to be careful when it became a torrent with eels and mullet pushing in the frontline of the water flow and froth. We had fun trying to grab them.

Shelly Beach was also a favourite. It's covered in thousands of little white shells. We had to wear sandshoes because of the poisonous devilfish that live in the sand. I liked swimming in the clear blue saltwater, fishing, looking for shells and coral, and picking up shellfish, called sand dollars, under the mangrove trees. We climbed these huge trees, and ate the mangrove nuts. No missionaries followed us in there, making it a magical place to escape.

One Tree Point is close to the mouth of the Gascoyne River. One time, me and Susan Samson and Beverley Pickett were having fun jumping up and down on the sandbar in the tidal creek among the mangroves. I wasn't watching where I was jumping and I landed in deep water. Luckily, one of the big girls, Aunty May Foley, was on the bank. She dived and saved me from drowning.

Peter Coppin loved these outings too. He always tried to duck me under the water. He was cheeky, but he had a good heart. Peter and me chased the jumping jack fish, trying to catch them, but we never could because they were too fast and slippery. At these places, the water was so clear you could see the bottom of the creek bed and all the fish swimming around you.

Yellowtail were delicious. Lynda James showed me how to cook them on hot coals without cleaning them — still with the scales on and the guts there. When the fish was cooked, we scraped away the scales that had kept the fish clean, and easily removed the insides that had rolled up into a ball. This is the best way to cook and eat fish, our old way.

The sea

Make sandcastles with cold wet sand
See them wash away, melt back to liquid sea
I need to sing with the whales floating free
Hear the music of the shells, waves and sea
Run with the salty wind, taste on the tongue
Stare at the big orange sun
Slowly drown into the black sea
Wait for sister moon under her dress of night
Look into my soul turned inside out
Oceans of history, rivers of tears
Mixed together to sort out my fears
Milky Way watch over me
Seven Sisters I can see
Stand near the midnight moon
Dreams drift and float through the cloudless night
Colours change into their uniform dull grey
I listen to the songs of this ancient land and sea
Their spirit flows over my heart and bones, over me
I am one with the land the rivers and the seas.

One morning, everyone except me had made their beds and had their aprons on. The fat cook, Balloon Bum, came around to check.

I lay there with the rugs up to my chin. I didn't know what was happening to me. There was blood on my sheets.

'What's wrong with you!' she bellowed. 'Why are you still in bed?'

With one great gesture, she bent down and pulled the covers off me. All the girls looked and saw blood everywhere.

I hated her. She didn't explain what was happening to me. She just turned to Lynda James and yelled, 'Tell her what to do!'

To this day, I feel real ashamed about how that missionary made everyone look at me, drawing attention to my condition.

But Lynda was good to me. She had a little sister named Marine at the mission, and maybe she became like a big sister to all of us. Lynda showed me how every month we had to go into the common room and make our own pads. I still didn't know why I was bleeding. Nobody told me. Later, I wondered how that mission lady told her own daughters. What did she say to them?

At the mission, we made our own fun with stories and dances. Under the shade of the two gum trees in the Senior Girls' yard, me and my special friend Susan Samson drew stories. Susan talked a lot, and she was a good storyteller. We filled a tin with water, and wet the ground. Then we sprinkled dry sand over the top. This was our storybook. We told yarns, drawing them as we spoke. Each time we rubbed it out, it was like turning a page. We sat for hours with sticks in our hands, telling our stories. Susan told me stories about her uncle who was a magic man. His favourite thing to do was to turn into a moth. After that, when a moth flew in, I would say, 'Hey, Susan! Your uncle's here to see you!'

Near the bough shed, a concrete mound was the perfect spot to balance and show off my dance moves. Susan traced my changing shadow in the dirt with her stick. I would do emu and kangaroo dance poses. I have always loved dancing. One time, I found a little book inside a magazine that showed the basic ballet positions. I hid in the toilets where no eyes could see, and practised my ballet steps, copying the pictures. These basic skills, and my love for dancing, have stayed with me.

One real hot Christmas Day in the mission yard, when I was about twelve, Miss Barton told us that we had to go on a treasure hunt for our present: 'Take five steps to that big gum tree ... Follow the arrow to the rock...'

We had fun racing around, following the instructions, and looking for the notes, excited about what surprise we would find at the end. The hunt took us from our yard all the way down to the school.

Finally, we found our gift. It was a pink bicycle. We were so happy. One bike for the Senior Girls, all forty of us. We booked our rides and knew who was on before us. I couldn't wait for my turn.

The big girls were riding it hard. Swinging it from side to side, trying to ride flash, and putting the style on. When it got to me, the tyre had a puncture. I missed out on riding our brand new bike, and had to wait till it was fixed. When it was repaired, we rode to see who had the best style. To this day, that is the only bike I've ever owned.

At other times, they gave us Christmas gifts in our pillowcases. Once, we got clear nail polish. Lynda and Marine James and me put some red watercolour paint in it, and painted our fingernails bright red. We got told off for being 'Jezebels'.

We never heard about Father Christmas, the Easter Bunny, or the Tooth Fairy. We were taught the Christian way.

Hairdressing has always fascinated me. Growing up, I often tried different hairstyles, and my most prized possession was that one purple hair roller — you know, the ones with elastic and a ball at the end to keep it in your hair. Every night I set my hair with this one hair roller. In the morning, in the Senior Girls' big bathroom mirror, I combed the fringe down and then got a pile of hair on top of my head, to make a nice smooth beehive style. To do this, you had to tease your hair, then smooth it out and hold it in place with bobby pins, standing your hair up high on your head. Then I'd do two kiss curls on the side of my cheeks. I was the only mission girl who ever wore her hair like that.

I remember one Sunday when we went to the Aboriginal reserve for church.

One of the elders frowned at me. 'What's wrong with your head, girl? Why do you have a big lump on it?'

Talk about laugh! I pushed down my hair to show that it wasn't a lump.

On my thirteenth birthday, the young missionary, Miss Barton, gave me a birthday present and card. The card read, 'Happy Birthday to the newest teenager in the world!' How thrilled I was! My present was a new pack of six purple hair rollers, and a thick purple belt, 1950s style. Now I owned seven hair rollers!

I raced into the bathroom. After shampooing my hair, dressing in my pyjamas, cleaning my teeth, and grabbing a comb to get the knots out, I raced back into the room to get my beautiful, new, purple hair rollers. One of the big girls strolled past me. My rollers were in her hair.

'Why have you got my rollers in your hair? They belong to me!' I screamed.

She smirked. 'These rollers are mine now.'

There was nothing to do. Crying wouldn't help, and no one would get them back for me. The kids would say, 'Rhonda Spratt you're a tell-tale tit, your tongue will split, and all the little puppy dogs will have a little bit.' I didn't want to be the centre of their teasing, so I went back to using that one hair roller, my prize possession.

At thirteen, I entered Teens Cottage where boys and girls could finally live together. Boys were up one end, and girls down the other. In its first year of operation, I was the youngest person there.

Mr and Mrs Finch were our new caretakers. Here, for the first time in my life, I was somebody's pet. I remember the day they arrived in a little green car. Mrs Finch was wearing a hairnet. I'd never seen a hairnet before. We called Mr Finch 'Mr Sheen' after the man on the furniture polish can because he was bald, short, and wore glasses, just like this character.

Mrs Finch cooked for us, and looked after me. She taught me how to make pastry flowers, toffees, scones, ice cream, mint lollies and marshmallows. She was also a wonderful gardener who loved gladioli. We had a beautiful garden filled with the colour and gentle fragrance of snapdragons, sweet peas, roses, flocks, gladioli and more. She also grew herbs that she used in our meals. Her mashed potatoes with buttermilk and chopped parsley tasted deadly. This was a new taste for me because we had never had herbs before. Every afternoon after school we sat together on the stool, and she played piano for me. In her younger days, she'd played piano for the silent movies.

In Teens Cottage, we no longer went to the big dining room; we made our own meals. One time while washing up, I forgot where I was and I started to sing.

'Stop, Rhonda!'

I felt a whack to the back of my legs and turned around.

'Stop singing, please. I've got a headache,' Mrs Finch said.

I kept singing. After Mrs Finch whacked me three more times, I kicked her back.

'Get up to the office!' She pointed the way.

Slowly, head hanging, I walked up to the office. After confessing my sin of singing while doing the dishes, I got the cuts with the cane from Mr Finch.

I refused to speak to either of them for weeks after that. After a while, they threatened to send me to a girls' home in Perth for not speaking. Not wanting to be sent away, I soon came out of my stubbornness, and started saying good morning to them again.

At the start of the following year, the older boys and girls left the mission. I often wondered where they went, and if they were all right wherever they were. I missed them, especially Lynda James who'd always made me feel safe.

With the older kids gone, girls my age came over to Teens Cottage, together with other boys. Ted was in this group. All through these years, we still hadn't had any time alone together — we were always watched. He did, however, show me how to play the guitar, teaching me three chords, a hymn, and a song by Slim Dusty.

One night, while the Finches were away, a young missionary lady came to care for us. Ted and me had come out first, and we were out the back of Teens Cottage. No one else was around. The washing was on the Hills Hoist, full of white sheets flapping away in the breeze. Ted grabbed my hand and we raced under the line.

We whispered as we stood side by side, holding hands, looking up at the stars. Ted told me the Aboriginal story about the Seven Sisters. He explained how they lived up in the Milky Way, and he tried to point them out to me. But the moon was too bright, so we couldn't see them clearly. He told me they were hiding behind that full moon. Next thing, our caretaker and all the other kids came outside wondering where we were.

'Where's Ted and Rhonda?'

They couldn't see us, cloaked by the sheets on the line.

We kept quiet. We hugged, and I had my first kiss.

Every Wednesday evening, the children were split up into groups for Christian Endeavour. Each week, a different child led these meetings. Ted and me were together in the same group. One time, our group was meeting at the mission school, a fair walk from our dormitories. While we were walking, I heard feet run up behind me.

'Come on! Let's go into the orchard here!' Ted grabbed my hand.

We didn't make it to the meeting. I was a bit scared as I'd never missed any meetings or church services. But there were no missionaries around, so I went with him. The orange, lemon and grapefruit trees were heavy with fragrant fruit. In the middle, a large fig tree stretched itself wide.

Ted and I chased each other around the orchard trees, picking up fallen fruits and throwing them at each other. We were having fun, but trying not to make too much noise. For a short while, we were just being teenagers, forgetting about prayers and rules.

A couple of times, a light came on in the dining room nearby. We laughed, and climbed the big fig tree. I was a good tree-climber back then. We had a good feed of figs. Then I started swinging off a branch.

Next minute, *crack!* I landed on my bum, still holding a branch full of fruit. The dining room light came on again. We could see the missionary peering out into the dark.

Ted came over and picked me up. He started tickling me, and we rolled around in the dirt, laughing. Then he gave me a big hug, and kissed me again. That's when I realised I was a girl and he was a boy.

Midnight magic

I gaze into the midnight sky
Milky Way so beautiful yet so long way away
Millions of sparkling stars I see
Looking back smiling at me

I witness a falling star dying
Fading quickly from the sky
Searching for a place to rest
From its place of high birth
To the dry dusty earth

The mopoke's lonely voice calls deep into the dim velvet night
Keeping us safe till the morning light
I am lost in the moment of magic
I feel my breath rise and fall
Life force is precious
Time short but free
The wonders of creation all around my feet below
All around my head above

I listen with my inner ear
To the music of the night
So crisp so gentle and so clear

Giving me peace, giving me love
Embracing my spirit, my very soul
Seeping, soaking deep within
The knowledge and wisdom for me to hold
The stars the earth
Giving me healing with new birth.

4

Finding country

One morning as I got off the bus to the town school, Cheryl Moncrief, a school-friend who lived on the fringes of East Carnarvon, came running, yelling that my mother was in town. I hadn't seen Mother since being put into the mission. Here I was in Grade Seven and twelve years old. All those years of silence. All those years of loneliness. All those years of wondering why.

As I lined up to go to class, my mind was turning over. Can this be true? I didn't know whether to believe Cheryl or not. We had been told our family was dead. I was too restless to do any schoolwork. I needed to go and find my mother, and I needed to do it now. Nervously, I raised my hand.

'Yes Rhonda, do you need something?' Our teacher was a kind and sporty young man.

'My mother's in town,' I whispered. 'Can I go and look for her please?'

Sitting on the edge of the chair, I held my breath and waited for his answer. Normally, to go downtown you had to have a note from the missionaries, and I didn't have one. Maybe I looked very sad because he responded, 'Yes.'

How exciting! At last I was about to see my mother.

I took off out of the classroom, through the school gates, past the convent, and down the street. But how would I recognise her? What did she look like? My mind was racing. What will I do? What will I say when I finally see her again? I hoped I didn't pass anyone because I might be passing her.

Finally, I reached the main street. I stood, catching my breath, and looked up and down the footpath, wondering what to do next. Who to ask?

I was in luck. Down the road, I spied Uncle Paddy Doka. Uncle Paddy was an elder who stayed on 'The Block' where my Nana Edna lived. The Block was a fair way out of town. You had to drive there.

Uncle Paddy had flowing white hair. He wore a white shirt, dark trousers and white sandshoes, even though he had no shoelaces. He looked frail, standing hunched over, holding both hands behind his back, trying to balance himself. When he heard me come running, he jumped with fright.

'Uncle Paddy! Hey, Uncle Paddy! Where's my mother?'

'Slow down, girl.' His dark eyes twinkled. 'Your mother's back at The Block with your Nana. I came into town with her husband.'

So it was true! She really was alive! Uncle Paddy wouldn't lie.

'That's her husband coming now.' Uncle pointed down the street.

I took one look at this man coming towards us, and got scared. He was a white man, and he was giant. Over six foot tall with white skin and blondish-red hair.

'My mother wouldn't marry an ugly man like that!' I cried.

As he got closer, panic set in. I had to get away.

'Don't tell him I'm here. Don't tell him who I am,' I whispered to Uncle Paddy. 'Please don't say anything.'

I ran into PJ's milkbar, and hid under a table with a long, white tablecloth. The two men stood in front of the shop talking for a minute or two. Meanwhile, here was me, peeping at them from under the tablecloth. Uncle Paddy gave me a sideways look. My finger touched my lips. 'Shhh.'

After a while they started heading down the street away from the shop. When it was safe, I crawled out of my hiding place. Scanning the scene, I watched as they climbed into a Land Rover. It was mustard yellow. They drove away. Uncle Paddy and the white man drove away, and they took my chance of seeing Mother with them.

I turned to start the slow walk back to school. My feet felt so heavy. My heart was breaking, and the lump in my throat was the size of a rock. I wanted to cry and cry. The pain was intense. Would Mother and me ever meet again? Tears wanted to come, but I fought them back. I fought them back strongly, like I had done my whole life. The world wasn't about to see my true feelings. I wasn't weak. I was a tough, strong, fighting mission kid.

As the school came into view, my emotions stayed under strict control. They were buried deep in the depths of my heart where no one could find them, and where they would stay forever. In the schoolyard, no one could tell how I felt. No one even bothered to ask. I was a good actor, putting on a fake show.

Then a thought came to me. Debbie would care! I raced around the schoolyard looking for my little sister to give her the good news. I found her and told her that our mother was in town and that I'd tried to see her.

'Stop telling lies!' she screamed. 'Our mother's dead!' She got louder. 'The missionaries told me our mother's dead! Our mother's fuckin' dead!'

She ran off. I stood there, stunned. Should I chase after her? I couldn't bear to see my little sister in such great pain. The school bell rang, bringing me out of my thoughts. The decision was made. I had to go back into class again.

That same afternoon, as usual, we all had jobs to do when we got back from school. This day, I was helping prepare the evening meal. Balloon Bum was in charge. My job was putting the mashed potato on all the plates. I stood by the window, on a stool because the pot was too big. A mustard yellow Land Rover drove past.

My heart started beating faster. Was this the same Land Rover I'd seen downtown when I was looking for Mother? Was it the same Land Rover that Uncle Paddy and the white man got into? My hopes started to grow. Could my mother be here to see me and my sister?

My questions were soon answered when one of the mission boys, Tommy Jones, came running in. 'Rhonda Spratt! Your mother's here to see you!'

Nervously, I started messing with my hair, taking out the piggy-tails I was wearing. Did I look all right? I wanted to look pretty for my mother.

I took a deep breath. 'Can I go and see my mother, please?'

'Carry on serving the potatoes,' Balloon Bum grunted. 'Your mother will have to come and knock on the door and ask to see you.'

I started serving the potatoes rough, just banging them on the plates.

Finally, a quiet knock hit the door.

'Can we see Rhonda?' a woman's voice asked. 'We were told she's working here in the dining room.'

Balloon Bum hit my shoulder. 'Rhonda, you can stop serving now, and go and see your visitors.'

With that, I was out the door.

Down the steps stood the giant, white man. My mother's sister, Aunty Inge, stood there too. I knew who she was because she had visited me and Debbie once and brought us a bag of grapes. In between them stood a beautiful lady who looked like me and my little sister. I guessed she was our mother. Aunty Inge stepped forward and smiled.

'Rhonda, this is your mother.'

My eyes glanced up, but my head stayed down. I wanted to throw myself into Mother's arms, but I was glued to the spot. I thought she would hold and cuddle me and say that she was here to take me and Debbie home with her for good. But none of that happened. My mother leant down and kissed me quickly on the cheek. She looked me in the eye. She had a beautiful face. Her eyes had a soft look, but they seemed a little sad. I was still waiting for her to tell me to go and get my stuff, so we could go home. I had seen another mother arrive and take her children home for good.

Then she introduced her husband to me as Uncle Stan. Silence. I had nothing to say. I had never had a voice. I hardly talked to the missionaries, so no voice of mine was ready to talk to them, my family.

And that was that. The moment I had waited years for was over in less than five minutes.

Next thing, I was back in the kitchen serving potatoes, and all the kids were chattering.

'Your mother is so beautiful,' they said.

The piano-playing missionary man came up to me. 'Now we know where you and your sister get your good looks from.'

I hated this man. I didn't like the way he said this in his smirky, sly way.

Lost child

Lost Dreaming, lost family
Lost land, lost language
Lost identity, lost me.

No one ever held me
to take away this killing sorrow.
That's stealing, taking away my soul.
I slowly drown in my tears
All alone with no helping hand

Missionaries' voices still haunt me
from so long ago
Jump out of my head
Jump out of my way

I never asked for this
To be stolen away
My heart was crushed
My body bruised
My spirit bashed and bent
My innocence brutally taken.

Can you hold my hand and never let go?
I need to know where I belong
Who can I trust? Where can I hide?
This feeling of emptiness, loneliness,
Echoes through the landscape of my mind.

Even though we grew up in different dormitories and played in different yards, Debbie and me knew we were sisters. She was cross with me, however, because I never took it up for her. 'Taking it up for someone' means that when someone wants to fight you, or is rowing with you, someone will step in and take your part. When someone had a fight with Debbie, she had to stand up on her own. I had to stand up on my feet, and I wanted her to do the same.

So, all her life, Debbie had to stand alone and protect herself against anyone who wanted to hurt or fight her. And there were a lot of fights at the mission. You had to show that you could fight, so they wouldn't pick on you. One day after school, while we waited for the second bus as the first one took the little kids back to the mission first, we were playing basketball. One of the big girls had picked all the other big girls for her team, leaving all the little girls for my team, including my sister. We were giving the big girls a good go, till a big one started picking on Debbie.

'Leave her alone! Leave Debbie alone!' I cried.

'Come here and say that! Come here, Rhonda Spratt, and say it to my face!' the big girl taunted.

So I fronted her. 'Just leave my little sister alone!'

With that, she took a swing to punch me. But I was quick and ducked away. I bounced up and upper-cutted her in the jaw. 'Fight! Fight!' the kids all ran over. We were going hit for hit. Debbie was scared. She held her hands over her face, thinking I would get flogged. She couldn't look. But then she peeped through her fingers, and saw that I was going okay.

While we were fighting, Ted walked past.

'Gee, Rhonda, you should get into fights more often. You look *real* beautiful when you're angry.' He grinned.

On the sideline, all the girls wanted to shout, but they were frightened. They cheered quietly, 'Come on Rhonda, come on Rhonda.'

That was the only time I took Debbie's part. But I've always been there on an emotional level for my sister. At the mission, I was her mother, her father, her sister, her brother. She has said I was everything to her.

Debbie has a good memory. Miss Barton, the young nurse with hairy legs under her long dresses, called Debbie a 'walking encyclopaedia'. One time, Miss Barton told Deb, 'If anyone's looking for me, tell them I've gone to the bank.'

A while later, someone asked where Miss Barton was.

'Oh,' Debbie replied knowingly, 'she's gone to the river.'

The missionary looked back puzzled.

When Miss Barton returned, the missionary asked her where she'd been. Miss Barton replied that she'd gone into town to go to the bank. The river bank was the only bank we knew; we didn't know about the money bank.

In my final year in Teens Cottage, Grade Ten at school, I was invited to spend the Christmas holidays with an Aboriginal girl's family at their cattle station. I was excited because this would be the first chance I had to live with Aboriginal people, not white people. Later, I learned that this family had wanted to set me up with their son. When their daughter found out that I was invited, she acted up.

'Well, if Rhonda Spratt goes, then I'm not going. I'll stay here!' she shouted.

This hurt me deeply. For the first time in my life, I fell to the floor and sobbed and sobbed. Before this, no one had seen my emotions; I cried where nobody could see. When my little sister found out, she started shaping up to fight this girl.

'What's ya problem, huh?' Debbie threatened.

Hearing all the noise, Mrs Finch came out. She took me aside into a dormitory and sat beside me on the bed.

'Why are you so upset, Rhonda?'

'I want to visit an Aboriginal family,' I said between sobs.

'Rhonda, don't you know where your mother is?' She looked concerned, but a bit surprised.

You should know, I thought to myself. I've been giving you letters to post to her for years. Those letters had the address on them.

I repeated the address to her: 'Mrs A. E. Webb, c/– Gogo Station via Fitzroy Crossing, West Kimberley, W.A.'

I thought nothing would happen after this, like it never happened when I never got any letters back from Mother. But this time, I was wrong. To my surprise, the missionaries contacted my mother, and they got a reply. A couple of weeks later, they told Debbie and me that we were going up north to where Mother was at Fitzroy Crossing. We could have holidays with her!

Flights were organised. We flew from Carnarvon to Port Hedland — just Debbie and me. We stayed there overnight with an Aboriginal family. Next morning, we flew to Derby. On that flight they served us a big chunk of bully beef, a hunk of damper, and a pannikin of tea. No plates or nothing. They must've thought we was drovers.

We spent the night in Derby where they put us up at the reserve. The Aboriginal family there gave us food and cared for us. We slept on the kitchen floor. I didn't want to leave. This was the first time in my life my own people surrounded me. Not a white face to be seen. I wanted to stay here at the reserve where I felt comfortable.

But it didn't last long. The next day, maybe because we were in flash clothes, the white Native Welfare Officer who lived across the road moved us into his family's house. We stayed with him until we caught the mail plane to Fitzroy Crossing. This little plane stopped at every cattle station. I was airsick for the whole trip. And to think, I had wanted to be an air hostess.

When we finally arrived at Fitzroy Crossing, my mother and stepfather stood there waiting. Mother wore a cool shift dress that she had made herself. She was as beautiful as I had remembered. It was good to see her and to be there. I got in the car and threw up all over the place again. I felt that embarrassed. As Mother wiped my face, she told me not to worry, that everything would be all right, and that she would clean everything up.

When we got to the house, Mother showed us where we would sleep. We met the other kids too, two more sisters and two more brothers.

'Be careful going to the toilet at night.' Mother pointed out back. 'A python visits, looking for its feed of green frogs.' She smiled.

It was good to be around Mother's energy and presence, and to know that I was a part of her. She made delicious bread and we ate a lot of beef too, as Gogo was a cattle station.

Years later, I learnt that Gogo was not far from another cattle property, Liveringa Station. My great-grandmother Nellie Spratt (born Male) was taken from Liveringa in the early 1900s and placed way down south at Moore River Native Settlement. So, a long way back, this is my family's Country.

Mother and the white man liked me. I liked her, but I wasn't sure about him. Debbie was more open. She started calling them 'Mum' and 'Dad' straight up. But it took me a long time to feel comfortable using those words. In fact, I never used the word 'Mum'.

Mother liked reading. Although she only went to school until Grade Three herself, she taught the Aboriginal kids from the camp reading and writing in the cave near her house. Mother also loved to fish. She asked us to catch green frogs for bait. I couldn't do it, though, because I liked the green frogs too much.

It was the wet season. One day, we went for a picnic to Geeky Gorge, a natural freshwater swimming hole that never dries up. There you can see blanket-fish; they're like stingrays.

I remember clearly that first picnic with the family. We shared sandwiches and then swam in the beautiful, fresh water. Later, we all walked along the high, sheer cliffs.

Towards the end of the day, it started with thunder, lightning and heavy rain. We ran into the mustard-coloured jeep. Us six kids jumped onto the two bench seats in the back and slid around all the way back to the house. That night, Mother cooked up chips with the fresh barramundi we'd caught. At home.

On my first holidays with the family, I felt awkward because, all our lives, we had worked and cleaned. Because my stepfather was the fill-in boss of several surrounding cattle stations, they had Aboriginal people coming in to do all the domestic jobs. Seeing them work while I did nothing made me feel slack, so I helped make the beds.

117

THE ABORIGINES ACT, 1905.

SECTION 12.

Regulation 12A (Form 10).

To THE COMMISSIONER OF POLICE and all Police Officers within the State of Western Australia.

WHEREAS it is deemed expedient by me, the undersigned, the Minister charged with the administration of "The Aborigines Act, 1905," that NELLIE SPRATT an Aboriginal, be removed to and kept within the boundaries of the MOORE RIVER NATIVE SETTLEMENT Reserve (or be removed from the ~~Reserve (or District) to the Reserve (or District) and~~ kept therein):

These are therefore to require you forthwith to arrest and apprehend the said NELLIE SPRATT, and ~~him~~ her to remove from the Perth Magisterial ~~Reserve~~ ~~(or~~ District), and safely convey within the boundaries of the MOORE RIVER NATIVE SETTLEMENT MOGUMBER Reserve (or District) and ~~him~~ her safely to keep within such Reserve (or District) during the Minister's pleasure.

Dated this 22nd day of April 1925

[signature]
for Colonial Secretary.

q 5506/28

Order to send Nellie Spratt to Moore River Native Settlement, 22 April 1925. Nellie was the mother of Rhonda's maternal grandfather, Clarrie Spratt.

I walked down to the Aboriginal camps too, and talked to the people. Their homes were built from tin — freezing cold in winter and stinking hot in summer. They asked me to read their medicine bottles so they could understand what their medicines were for, and how much to take.

I had always put my mother on a pedestal. I thought she was perfect in every way because I never knew or saw her. One night though, Mother went into town. When she got back, she was drunk. The other kids were giving her cheek, and she chased them around the yard with a switch. I fell to the grass in the dark and wept. My mother wasn't an idol. She had a drinking problem. Mother had grown up in Moore River, and had probably gone through many similar experiences to me. Now that I'm an adult I can understand how she came to drinking that way, but at the time it shocked me to think that she needed this. She had fallen off that pedestal. Even so, she was still my mother, and I still loved her — not that I could show her. In later years, Mother gave up drinking and smoking. To me, this showed her courage and strength of will and mind. These are her gifts to me.

In the middle of summer during the wet season, everybody comes to Gogo Station for Lore Time. Lore Time is a traditional tribal gathering where mothers hand their boys over to the men before initiation into manhood. Initiation is carried out among men only, away from the eyes of women. My brothers and sisters explained that, as part of Lore Time, we were having a big corroboree, and that this gathering was for everyone: men and women.

That beautiful star-filled evening, among the spinifex and anthills, in a clearing between our family home and the camp, we all sat around two large, sacred fires. The women sat on one side, and the men on the other. Glowing by the firelight, I smelt the earth, listened to the clapping of hands and clapsticks, and the chanting of ancient songs, and felt the rhythm of stamping feet — the Dreaming surrounding me.

Women got up and danced in a line, holding each other's waists. They invited us to get up and join them. Men danced on their side around their own fire.

There is one vision from that night I will never forget. A very fit Aboriginal man stood in the centre by the fire, holding two boomerangs in his hands above his head. His lean brown body glowed as he performed the rainbow snake dance. He moved like a snake, and the light of the fire flickered on him. It was a powerful image that my eyes were fixed on.

Being a part of this ceremony affected me deeply. Sitting on Mother Earth with Aboriginal people and their music as ancient as this land, I was lost in a good way, at one with my culture on this red ground.

Then tiredness hit me. Apparently, corroborees go all night from the Evening Star to the Morning Star. But I wanted to go home. Nobody had told me the protocols, so I left. No one stopped me. The next day, they said I should have stayed. Not growing up with culture or Lore, I didn't know.

After a week with my mother, it was time to leave. I wanted to stay with her, but it wasn't up to me. Native Welfare controlled my life. I was sixteen, so it was time for them to send me to Perth to start my hairdressing apprenticeship.

5

Scared in the city

In 1967, the Minister from the Churches of Christ in Fremantle came to visit the mission. Mrs Finch told him that I was interested in hairdressing. He remembered that one of his parishioners owned a hairdressing salon, and he promised to ask her if she would have me as an apprentice. Shortly after, we received word back that Miss Ball was willing to give me a go. So, at the end of that school year, I would leave the only place I knew as home.

Before leaving, Ted and me found a way to meet secretly, one last time. He told me he had something for me.

'I hope you'll be all right in the city,' he said.

He pulled $40 out of his pocket, and pressed it into my hand.

'Where'd you get all this?' I looked at him.

'Working at Brickhouse Station.'

I quickly took the money and hid it deep in my skirt pocket. We shared one last hug.

MG:WOODS.
NORTH WEST.
CARNARVON.
21/11/1967.
CN:12-1-1
NWG: 12-1-1.

Supt. of Native Welfare,
North West Division,
Box 33, Post Office,
PORT HEDLAND. 6721.

Re: Girls to Employment.

I have been advised by the Carnarvon Mission that have been accepted for positions in Perth.

Rhonda Spratt (17.8.1951) is the other who is to be employed for training by a Hair Stylist of Fremantle. Rhonda is to commence employment any time after the 27th of this month. Her wage will be $8.00 per week for the first six months. She will be living with a private family (name unknown at present) and will pay board of $8.00 per week plus fare to and from work of $1.80 per week.

I would request advice in regard to departmental assistance in respect to fares to Perth, clothing allowance, and particular the latter case whether assistance under instruction B-7-3 would apply.

Rhonda Spratt was placed in the Mission by for training and schooling. The department however had subsequently seen fit to approve of a special subsidy in this case, and to date there has been no

It would not appear that even the fare to Perth for the girl could be issued on a recoverable basis, and as previously mentioned further assistance will especially apply in this case for clothing, and possible subsidization of wages.

Could and early advice be forwarded on these matters please.

Full details will be supplied of both to Central Division when they are sent to Perth.

Letter dated 21 November 1967 that outlines how Rhonda would be sent to a hair salon for employment. The letter seeks a government subsidy as all of her wages would go to her foster family for board. Details of who took Rhonda to the mission and why have been erased, together with an explanation for why the government approved a special subsidy for her. As provided by FOI, Dept. Child Protection, WA, decision date: 27 March 2013.

It was scary — the thought of leaving what I'd known all my life to go to the big city, far away, far from my little sister and all the mission kids who were my family. Whenever I got the cane, I'd shout at the missionaries, saying that I couldn't wait to leave this stinking place; that I hated it here and would never ever come back. But, as the bus pulled away, I turned to grab one last look before the mission vanished into the distance. I wanted to cry, but didn't.

My new journey into the unknown took me to Perth then Fremantle, miles away down south. It was a culture shock, being sent to stay with strange city people.

Arriving at this first place, I gave the lady of the house the $40 that Ted had given me. I had never kept anything of mine before, so I didn't know that keeping the money was possible. She said casually that she would 'keep it for a rainy day'.

I thought to myself that I would have a very long wait for the money because we were in the middle of summer, and it wouldn't rain until winter time. I can look back now and laugh, but at the time it was very confusing.

Up until then mission life was the only life I knew. We did everything to the mission bell. Here in the city, there was no mission bell or missionaries telling me what to do. It was very strange having my own room too. All my life, noisy dormitories with lots of kids had filled my head. I felt all alone in my new room.

My first day at work in Wenda Salon was scary. Dressed in a white uniform with white shoes and a red cardigan, I was real shy. Because of my dark skin, I felt that people could see me a mile away. My hair was cut very short, like Mia Farrow, but black in colour.

But my boss, Miss Gwen Ball, was a kind and caring person. She gave me the opportunity to learn a trade. Fresh out of school, and not knowing the ways of the world or anything about beauty treatments, I had no idea about the life I was stumbling into — a life of money and time, tints and perms, waxing and manicures, shampoos and blow waves, sets and hairspray.

Here in the workforce, far away from my known world, I felt self-conscious and afraid. My wage was $8 a week, and my board was $8 a week. They only gave me 50 cents for Jesus on Sunday. Nobody here looked like me. In the mission, we outnumbered the white people. Where were all the Aboriginal people? I didn't want to be here, but had no choice. I didn't want to stand out, but blending in was impossible.

As I changed into the uniform, one of the white girls called out, 'Look at you! You're so skinny!'

Another teased, 'Look at your ribs. I can pluck a tune on them!'

I didn't say anything, and kept getting dressed.

Miss Ball told me to write down my start time, lunch time and finish time. I could hardly read a clock, but managed to work it out with the help of some clients. Writing out our clients' bills, taking their money, and giving back the correct change were also my jobs. I'd never handled much money before; I'd only held a penny or a two-bob coin. Early on, while serving a lady, I accidentally pulled the whole till drawer out. Coins and notes flew everywhere. After that, I couldn't think properly. I asked her if she could help me count out the change for her.

My other duty was answering the phone. The phone frightened me, so, when it rang, I disappeared to the other section of the salon, and hoped that someone else would answer it. But Miss Ball always buzzed me to come and pick it up.

In a slack way, I would answer, 'Ullo. What? You want your 'air done? Is that for an 'aircut? And 'oo you want to cut your 'air?'

Miss Ball's mother told me that that was no way to speak on the telephone. A few weeks later, she rang the salon. She thought it was one of the white girls speaking. I had soon learnt how to speak flash English.

Some of the white boys in the street, who didn't even know me, made fun of me, calling me 'Rinso Girl'. Rinso was a brand of laundry powder. Maybe they said that because my white clothes looked even whiter against my dark skin. Any other time, I would have stamped up to these boys and told them to shut their traps. But, in this new place, it seemed like my fighting spirit had gone. I was sixteen years old, and stunned by this white city world.

Searching faces in the streets looking for any other Aboriginal person was no use; there weren't any. In the late 1960s, I felt like the only blackfulla in the whole of Freo. This was the only time in my life that I wished I was white. I wanted to blend in and not be seen, not be different.

One time, during my lunch hour, someone shoved and pushed me so fiercely in my back that I fell down onto the hard street, flat on my tummy, hurting my knees and hands.

'You don't belong here, so fuck off!' an angry man's voice shouted.

Tears came to my eyes. I swallowed hard. No one stopped to help me. It was like I was invisible, like nothing had happened. Slowly, I picked myself up, and looked to see who had done this to me. But everyone just carried on with their business, walking like zombies in a trance, trapped in their own world.

After that, during lunch I sat in our dark, poky lunchroom with two workmates. I was too shy and nervous to know what to say. They sat opposite me, close together, eating and whispering to each other, and giving me sideways looks.

One day, they were down the other end, talking and giggling.

'Are you a virgin?' one of them started.

I thought they wanted to talk with me and include me now.

'Yes. I'm a Christian!' I eagerly replied.

All my life we had heard about the Virgin Mary, so I thought this question had to do with religion. They turned to each other, giggling, and began whispering again. But I didn't care. I didn't want to talk anyway.

Down the track, when a particular client and me got to know each other well, I plucked up some courage.

'Can you tell me what a virgin is?' I asked her.

'A virgin is someone who hasn't had sex,' she replied straight up.

On finding out what the word meant, I just exploded. I was so wild. How dare these girls ask me that!

In my rage, I forgot about doing my client's hair. I just wanted to get even. Picking up rollers, brushes, clips, anything my Yamatji hands could find, I let rip. Things went flying through the air every which way. I didn't care; I wanted to get them. The girls were dodging, ducking and hiding, so they wouldn't get hit. A lump rose in my throat. Tears and screams wanted to bust out, and I wanted to go back home, wherever that was.

But before anyone could see me cry, I raced out of the salon, down the two sets of stairs, past the Wesley church, and headed for the park opposite the train station. There I sat and cried. Some old men were playing chess on a table under a palm tree. The sky was blue and the grass was green, but I didn't care. Why couldn't I be with people like me? Blackfullas.

I didn't want to be different, and I didn't want to be called the 'dear little Aboriginal girl' or 'Rinso Girl' anymore either. I was sick and tired of everything, and I wanted to be white. Then no one would notice me, no one would pick on me, and I would just blend in and be like every other person in the salon and on the streets of Fremantle.

With all these thoughts flying through my mixed-up mind, I didn't realise that my boss had followed me to the park. Miss Ball sat down beside me, and put her hand on my shoulder.

'What's the matter, dear?'

I couldn't answer her. She took my hand and we walked back to the salon in silence.

My boss was tall and slim with a thin face, thin nose, and short, thinning hair. But there was nothing thin or short about her patience, her heart, or her kindness.

As part of my five-year hairdressing apprenticeship, once a week I studied at TAFE. I consider finishing my hairdressing apprenticeship as one of my greatest achievements. During my final exam, all the examiners were standing in a group, staring at me, and mumbling. After everything was done, my teacher came over.

'Rhonda,' he said smiling. 'We've just been discussing what mark we should give you. You got 100 per cent on your test, but we decided that no one is perfect, so we'll give you ninety something.'

Long before this though, after a few weeks at TAFE, and after getting to know the other girls, I started to talk. During lunch hour one day, a student announced that she was getting her cat sterilised.

'What!' I said, shocked. 'You're going to boil your cat? That's so cruel.'

She just gave me a funny look and didn't explain. All the other girls laughed.

That evening, at my first foster family's house, I shared the story with them. The whole table went quiet. Their white faces turned pink. What had I said? No one explained that sterilising was an operation to stop the cat from having babies.

Each Sunday after breakfast, this family headed to church. Here I was again, singing hymns, reading the Bible, praying, and putting money on a plate. After church, we returned to their house for a roast meal and sweets. After dinner had settled, we went for a Sunday drive around Fremantle and bought ice creams. I liked ice cream, and this foster father was good to talk to. He was kind and gentle, and he always bought me chocolate ice cream, my favourite.

During these drives, we passed signs that read 'Natives for Sale'. I thought they were going to sell me off. I closed my eyes and wished hard, 'Please don't turn in, please don't turn in.' Down the track, I realised that these places weren't selling our people; they were selling native plants. It was disturbing. We Aboriginals came under the Native Act. We were called 'natives', just like these plants.

After work on Saturdays, I caught a train into Perth to meet up with Debbie and Ted who were staying in girls' and boys' Aboriginal hostels there. Ted and me kept in touch through writing love letters each week.

From the train station, I walked to Mount Lawley, passing by Beaufort Park. Many Aboriginal elders gathered there. Often, as I passed them, they stopped me. I would always acknowledge them with a smile and a hello.

'Are you Alice's daughter?' they asked.

They had grown up on Moore River Native Settlement where my mother had grown up. Apparently, I am the mirror image of my mother. It happened too many times to count. It felt nice because people recognised me, or at least they recognised my mother in me. It made me feel good because, all my life, I had wondered who I looked like. And here were these strangers asking, 'Are you Alice's daughter?'

While staying with the first foster family, I asked to go to night school to study my Leaving English and to learn cake decorating. So, twice a week, after work and tea, I attended South Fremantle Technical College. I was the only Aboriginal person in class. To get to both courses, I had to walk, no matter the weather. When it rained, many times I was the only wet person sitting in class. I felt slack, sitting there cold and wet, but, wanting to learn, I put these feelings on hold.

I studied these two subjects for a year. Cake decorating was fun. I even learnt how to decorate a Dolly Varden cake. Being creative came naturally to me. On the other hand, English was a struggle. I had to put my head down and my mind to work. For me, it's much easier to tell a story than write one. Anyway, I stuck with English and, at the end of the year, I sat exams at the University of Western Australia and passed.

Late one night, walking back to the house from night school, it was just me, the footpath, the trees and the streetlights. Suddenly, a car revved up slowly behind me. It was a main road, so it was strange that this car was going so slow. It got closer and closer. A carload of young white fellas stopped near the footpath behind me. Seeing them, I got scared. My heart beat faster.

'Want a lift?' one called out.

My head stayed down, and I picked up my pace.

A car door opened and footsteps ran towards me. Panicked, I started to run, but his breath was panting closer behind my neck.

Then he grabbed me. I struggled against his grip, but he was too big and too strong. He clasped my waist, pinning my arms down, and picked me up in a bear hug. I was sixteen years old and weighed eight stone. He was massive and very strong.

I was frozen by fear. Something bad was going to happen for sure. He threw me into the car. A spider's web of waiting arms and legs trapped me. The sour smell of beer and cigarettes filled my nose. What could I do? There were too many of them and only one of me.

'I only live around the corner. Could you drop me off there?' I asked uselessly.

They ignored my plea and drove straight past my place. Hope was fading.

Next thing, the car turned down a dirt track. We bumped along, further into a lonely, dark pine forest — no shops, no buildings, no streetlights.

They're going to kill me, I thought, and there's nothing I can do about it. I was outnumbered and powerless, terrified and sobbing.

With a knife to my neck, they brutally raped me, over and over again. With their teeth they bit me, with their fists they punched me, with their open hands they slapped me, with their feet they kicked me, and with their clenched hands they tore clumps of hair from my scalp. No one heard my screams.

Throughout the terror, I wanted to die. I wished hard that they would slice my throat with that knife. The nightmare and torment seemed like an eternity.

When they had finished with me, they dragged me out of the car and dumped me on the ground, like I was nothing. They sped off, leaving me alone on the floor of the pine forest.

My body was bruised and battered, my dress was ripped, my spirit was smashed, and my heart was broken.

'Mummy, Daddy! Mummy, Daddy!' I called out hugging my knees to my chin, rocking back and forth, just as all of us mission kids had done growing up, whenever we were scared or hurt. But, as it had been all my life, despite my calls, nobody came to comfort me.

I sat there for a while with just the forest noises and pine scent surrounding me. I had to be strong. My strength came from the earth. The earth has never let me down. She is always there for me, giving me comfort. She helped me realise quickly that I had better get going, because they might return.

Thankfully, it was a full moon, so I could see where my jumper and shoes lay. Softly sobbing and shaking, I rushed over, gathered my clothes, and wrapped my jumper around my torn dress. Normally, I'm afraid of the dark, but here, alone in the night, because the criminals had left, I felt strangely safe.

I rose to my feet and staggered slowly down the dirt track. The forest was about two miles from my house, and I had to pass the cemetery. Cemeteries had always scared me, as spirits of the dead had always frightened me. But this night, I realised that dead people can't hurt you like the living, so my fear vanished.

Stumbling into the house, I didn't want anyone to see me. The front door opened quietly, and, when I entered, the family were all in the lounge room watching TV. They called out to greet me.

I murmured back, gathered my pjs, and headed straight to the bathroom. For me, the warm running water was soothing and comforting. It was the hug that I needed. I stood under the shower trying to cleanse myself; trying to wash away all the hurt and pain, their mean words, smell and touch — to make myself clean. In the shower, you could cry, and no one could hear you. It was a safe place.

I didn't tell the family that night. I just went to bed early. In fact, I didn't tell anybody ever, until now. I had no intention of telling white fullas ever because I felt that no one would hear me or believe me. So that little sixteen-year-old Rhonda has carried this festering wound around with her for half a century.

I knew that I needed medical help, but didn't turn to people for assistance as no one had ever cared for me. I felt alone again. Like always, I handled this by myself. I really needed love at this time — someone who would listen and believe me. Someone who would tell me that everything was okay, that they loved me for me, and not for what they could take from me. But, because I didn't have a voice, my true feelings were shared with no one.

The evil pack of criminals didn't physically murder me, and my wounded body gradually healed, but their vicious attack committed first-degree murder on my soul. After that night, my trust, confidence, love of life and mental health were all shattered. And the very essence of me has never fully recovered. Even after all this time, those events still linger, haunting me when I least expect it. I wish that part of my memory could be wiped out for good and made bankrupt, so it cannot torment me anymore.

Maybe I should return to that pine forest in bright sunlight and search for my innermost being. When I find my very self, that young innocent girl lying naked, murdered and exposed on the forest floor, I'll lovingly gather her up, hold her tight, and gently return her home.

On another occasion, this group of thugs came back and did this to me again. An Italian gang dragged me off the streets twice as well.

Why was life so vicious and cruel? I didn't want to be a part of it anymore. All it had offered me was misery and despair. Was I only put on this earth for white men to abuse me? Because that was all they had done so far.

Looking back, I can't believe that my emotional wellbeing survived. As a child, I had learned to block out my true feelings. Here I was now doing it all over again. I never showed how I was drowning inside. But, sometimes, a tidal wave of unshed warm, salty tears threatened to pull me into the deep, dark depths of overwhelming sorrow. I feared it would drown the real me forever. Somehow, by the skin of my teeth, I managed to struggle to the surface and live — but only just.

Night

Night is here again,
it's dark and cold outside and in,
and I'm all alone

My company is the TV that I vacantly stare at
Not really hearing, not really seeing, not really there
The endless sound of the clock never stops — tick, tock
Echoes slowly through the valleys of my mixed-up lonely mind

My hands and feet are cold and numb
Streetlight seeps dimly through the damp window pane
Crickets gather to sing night-time songs
Sadness is creeping, tiptoeing, seeking,
Finds my body, floods through my skin
to my bones, to my core

I want to hide, run, escape, but now it's too late
It finds me and kills my trust, hope and dreams
I am empty, dead from the inside looking out.

6

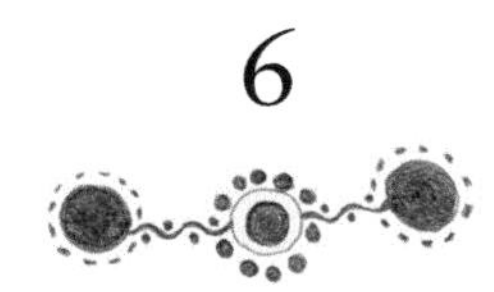

A family at last

During my first four years in Perth, I lived with three white foster families. I ran away from the second one. One night Sylvia, my workmate who lived just a couple of streets away, came around to the foster family's house and invited me to watch TV at her place. Where I was staying, they had no TV.

'If you step out the front door, don't bother about coming back!' the lady of the house threatened.

I thought they didn't want me to stay there anymore. After I finished watching TV with Sylvia's family that night, I left their place. Not knowing where to go or what to do, and just with the clothes on my back and $8 in my pocket, I walked away into the night. I caught a bus into Freo, and walked around till dawn. I took the first morning train into Perth, heading for Beaufort Park where I knew many Aboriginal people gathered.

All day and half the night I sat there until an Aboriginal family came and took me in. Down the track, I found out that this Nyungar lady had the same name as my father's family; she was a Ugle. The very next day, because of my strong work ethic, I caught the train back to Fremantle to the hair salon. That same day, the boss asked me for my new address.

While we were having dinner that night, there was a knock on the door. Standing on the porch were six white men. Five were detectives, and one was a Christian man who I remembered seeing at the mission. He used to come up for his holidays and hand out lollies to the children. Even though I wanted a lolly, I always stood off in the distance.

'Rhonda,' the detective said, 'as a ward under the Native Act, you are breaking the law by not living with your legal guardian.'

I stood and stared at all these men in uniform.

'You have two choices,' he went on. 'Either go with these detectives and myself back to the station, or go with Mr Taylor here from the church.'

Because Mr Taylor was familiar and I knew he had Aboriginal kids at his house, I decided to go with him. Slowly, I gathered my things together and slumped into his car. On the way to his place, I sobbed.

Mr Taylor pulled over at a garage and asked what was wrong.

'Well, really,' I said, 'I don't want to go with any of you. I want to stay with the Aboriginal family. I don't want to go to your house because you'll make me go to church three times on a Sunday, and I'm sick of it.'

Mr Taylor took a long breath. 'Let's make a deal then,' he said. 'On Sunday, you don't have to go to all the services, just pick one. That's all I ask of you.'

So that was the deal I agreed to.

When we got to his house, it was good to see Aboriginal kids. I hadn't seen any of my mob for a long time. There were seven of us and three of Mr Taylor's own children.

Mrs Taylor had worked hard all her life and looked old for her age. Walking stooped over, and always wearing an apron and glasses, she looked more like a grandmother than a mother.

It turned out Mr and Mrs Taylor were caring and wonderful human beings. In the bathroom, however, a strap hung from the mirror.

Oh, no! That's what he's going to hit us with! I thought.

One day, passing the bathroom, I saw Mr Taylor sharpening his razor on that strap. Always well dressed, he was shaving for his workday as an undertaker.

'I thought you were going to flog us with that,' I said quietly.

He told me that every mission kid who'd stayed there had told him the same thing. He never flogged us, nor spoke a harsh word, and his patience was endless, but Mr Taylor did use reverse psychology on us.

'You can go out,' he'd say, 'but you know I'm not happy about you going.'

That would wreck our night.

Mrs Taylor was a great cook and a deadly dressmaker. When they were in season, she bought lots of stone fruits and stewed and bottled them, sitting all the jars of different colourful fruits along the top of the kitchen cupboard. She made our dresses too. Somehow she managed to feed and clothe ten children.

A couple of days after moving in with the Taylors, I was called up to front Mr Stirling. He was on the Board of the Aboriginal Churches of Christ. Mr Stirling had been Superintendent at the mission. He was also the first person to give me a hiding, when I was in kindergarten.

Me and my friend Susan Samson had gotten into the chookyard. We were making mudcakes with real eggs, just like we'd seen the missionaries do in the kitchen. When they caught us, the dormitory workers lifted us up by our braces and frog-marched us into Mr Stirling's office. If you went to the office, you knew you would get a hiding. Mr Stirling caned us hard across our backs and legs. We were only about four years old.

Now, here I was all grown up and once again standing in his office, wondering what was going to happen. I didn't get a hiding this time, but his words were just as hard-hitting and painful like the cane.

'Rhonda, you'll never make it,' Mr Stirling fumed across his big, wooden desk. 'You'll never fit into white society. You will be a drunk and a no-hoper. You'll be in the gutter, like all your family.'

Is this what he really thinks of me and my people? I thought. I wanted to scream at him. But it was like they had taken all that away from me — my voice, my identity, my strength. Because I wasn't following the rules set down for us, this is what he spoke to me.

Since then, when I have any self-doubt, Mr Stirling's evil words invade my head. I tell them to go away because I didn't end up like that. I've never been in the gutter, I've never let alcohol be my boss, and I *want* to be like my family because I am proud of each one of them. I never saw Mr Stirling again after that day, but I've often thought of him and his nasty words.

Shortly after that incident, I tried to take my life. I thought nobody cared. Why walk on this earth? I thought. Maybe I am better off under the ground.

But Mr Taylor was helpful and kind, and I grew to trust him. Our people often rang him up, and he gave them food and transport. Every night, both Mr and Mrs Taylor came into our rooms to give us a hug goodnight, but I always pulled away.

One time, when they were away for the evening, I was washing up.

'Why don't we go for a run around the block?' I suggested to one of the other girls.

Next thing, *whack!* Something hit me from behind, knocking the wind right out of me. Another foster kid had grabbed a huge pot and struck me in the back. Maybe she reckoned I was suggesting the run because she was a bit fat.

I turned around, flung off my dishgloves, and was into it. Next I knew we were under the table, rolling around. Soon one of the boys came in and got me in a bear hug from behind. I grabbed this girl the same way and wouldn't let go. Luckily, Mr and Mrs Taylor arrived home, broke us up, and sorted it out.

If it was somebody's birthday, Mrs Taylor always baked a cake. One evening, a beautiful fruitcake with almonds around the top edge sat gleaming on the dinner table. After the meal, only me and their daughter Bernice were left. Before taking the first lot of plates off the table, I thought I'd steal an almond off the top of that cake.

'Don't do that!' Bernice turned, and her long blonde plait flicked her cheek.

I ignored her, grabbed an almond, and took the first lot of plates into the kitchen. Returning, I thought to myself, I enjoyed that first almond so much, I'll have another one.

'Don't touch that cake!' the white girl screeched again.

Ignoring her once more, I claimed my treat and continued clearing the dining room table. After taking in that lot of dishes, I came back for the third load. Collecting the plates and cups, I thought, I'm going to grab a third almond now.

On seeing this, the girl lost it. 'I told you not to take that almond!'

With that, I just exploded. Cups, plates and knives flew up and soon lay smashed and scattered across the floor. Then, something inside me really snapped. Without a word, I walked around to her and, with all my might, I smacked her across the face. I hit her so hard that her nose broke. Nose went one way, blood went the other.

Realising what I'd done, I ran out the front door into the cold, wet winter's night, wearing only my white work uniform. I raced up the hill, looking back to see if they were following me. As I reached the top, the lights of Mr Taylor's car started heading towards me. He was soon by my side. Calmly, he told me to come back home.

'No!' I cried. 'I've hurt your daughter, so you'll probably all hate me now.'

We began a tug-of-war on the footpath. As I struggled to pull away from him, a car pulled up. The driver asked if I was all right.

'It's okay,' Mr Taylor reassured him. 'It's a family problem.'

The man drove on. I pleaded with Mr Taylor to just let me go.

'Where will you go, Rhonda?' he asked.

'I don't know. I'll just keep running.'

I was sure they wouldn't want me anymore, and felt miserable because I'd finally found a place where people cared for me. But even though his daughter was seriously hurt, Mr Taylor didn't scream at me. He continued to ask me to come out of the rain and go back home with him in the car. Feeling wet and cold, I finally decided to go back with him now, and leave later.

When we got back to the house, Mrs Taylor and their daughter stood waiting at the front door. To my amazement, they hugged me. Bernice told me that everything was okay. She said she forgave me while sniffling through her nose, all bleeding and bent.

By their actions, the Taylors taught me more in that moment than I'd learnt from all my childhood preachings at the mission. Even today, that episode still affects me. Because of three almonds I ate, I got to see their true spirits. The Taylors lived up to what they believed in.

After leaving the mission, Debbie and me wrote to each other. In time, she came down to Perth to secretarial college. After she graduated, she worked with a major film distributor and lived in one of the Aboriginal girls' hostels. I often visited her and we played in the same all-Aboriginal basketball team.

One year we made the grand final and played at Perry Lakes Stadium. During the game, however, all the girls in our side were fouled off, leaving just me and Debbie against a full team. We dealt with a lot of racism, even from the umpires. We could have beaten that team if all our players were still on.

Debbie has told me since that she secretly dreamed of being a professional basketball player. But most of all she dreams of turning back time, so that she doesn't have to live with all the scars and trauma she carries.

In 1970, during NAIDOC (National Aborigines and Islanders Day Observance Committee) Week, at the age of nineteen, I headed out to the Aboriginal Ball at Perth's town hall. Mrs Taylor had sewn me a beautiful, soft pink dress with pleats and a diamante belt. Mr Taylor dropped me and some other kids off. What a sight! It was amazing to see all the Aboriginal people in their suits and gowns. The music and chatter of blackfulla voices provided a wonderful atmosphere. Here I belonged.

On the dance floor, one man stood out from the crowd. What a good-looking fulla he is, I thought. But even though he'd seen me too we didn't speak.

I didn't think about him again until the next day when he rocked up at my foster home with his cousin Betty. This girl lived in Fremantle, and I'd met her at a church meeting.

So, Jerry Collard and me started going out. Our first date was at the Claremont Speedway. Jerry is Nyungar nation of the Balladong tribe with bloodline connections to the Onslow area and the central desert. He's a moorditj man; tall, with long eyelashes. He reminded me of the actor Omar Sharif. In fact, Arabs often came up to Jerry, talking in Arabic.

When we met, Jerry was a seasonal worker, living and working at Brookton, over two hours' drive inland from Perth. He worked on farms, shearing, and clearing and ploughing the land for wheat. We wrote letters to each other. For the first time, my mail came to me directly without someone else opening and reading it first. Every weekend, Jerry came up in his ute to visit. Jerry was real good at farmwork, and sport too. He played cricket and football for his hometown.

Sometimes, I travelled to Brookton and spent time with Jerry and his family. He had grown up with his family. His mother and grandfather were both blind from diabetes. Being the youngest, Jerry cared for his parents, Lottie and George Collard.

I got jealous of them having each other, having that close family connection that was totally foreign to me. My jealousy caused a lot of problems. I didn't mean to be unkind, but I didn't know how to show love. To see it happen in front of your eyes, to be around someone who'd grown up in a loving family, this to me was overwhelming. This love among mother, father and son was a treasure I envied and, although I understood this, it upset me that I'd never had unconditional love with my own family. Those bonds had been broken through no choice of my own.

One weekend on our way to Brookton, we detoured to the town of Beverley. Jerry had discovered that some of my family lived there on the native reserve. When we arrived, my Grandfather Clarrie's brother, Jack — yes, Jack Spratt — was pleased to see me.

'I've got a photo of your mother!' Jack shouted.

He raced into his house and brought out a photo to give me.

Years later, I showed my mother this photo.

'That's not me. That's my grandmother, Nellie Male,' she smiled.

Mother explained that Nellie, her father's mother, was born at Snake Creek on Liveringa Station in the Kimberleys. She was Gidja (or some say Kija). As a child, Nellie was taken by a white man to Moore River Native Settlement far away south from where she was born. She managed to somehow return to Liveringa for a while. But in 1925 Nellie was sent back to Moore River under police guard 'as she may want to break away', the government memo warned.

I still have that photo of my great-grandmother who was stolen, just like me. Nellie looks like both me and my mother. It was good to meet a group of Spratts because in the mission there had only been me and Debbie.

Two years later, Jerry and me got married. Driving along one day, I told him that when I finished my hairdressing apprenticeship I wanted to go back home. He pulled over the ute and asked me right then and there if I would stay and marry him instead. We had grown to love each other.

But our life together wasn't easy. From our honeymoon night on, we always had Jerry's family staying with us. We never had time to ourselves. This was a shock to me because I only knew the white world where married couples live without extended family under the same roof.

One day, things came to a head and I threatened to leave. From then on, we got our own little flat in Fremantle. It was close to work and, by this time, Jerry had joined the police force. Because we were now married, Jerry decided he needed a steady job. He became one of the first two Aboriginal policemen in Western Australia.

Jerry was a good provider. He bought the stores, he paid all the bills, and we always had a roof over our heads and food on the table. But we had our ups and downs like all people in life. Jerry often said that I was like a rock that was dead inside because I couldn't show any feelings.

'Why can't you cry when you feel sad? You have a heart of stone. Just show me something!' he pleaded.

After a life of hiding how I felt, even though I loved him, I couldn't bring myself to let Jerry see the real me. Jerry turned out to be the love of my life.

Emotionally dead

Emotionally dead
Socially unwanted
No need to suffocate
I need to communicate

No sense of belonging
No sense of who I am
Lost in this world of confusion
Cold and hungry

Come take me away to the rainforest
Warm, damp and sweet
Need time to heal the broken soul
Find love and belonging
in this pollution of life
Don't want this isolation

Take my hand and hold me
Let me know the beauty of touch.

I tried as hard and as long as I could to show Jerry how much I cared for him and our two children, John and Lisa.

Our son John has been here before; he's an old spirit. He could talk before he could walk. At age three, he could recite poetry and sing. John is a gentle person with a gentle soul. We lived in Greylands, a suburb of Perth, when he was little. Out the back was a migrant hostel. Somehow, John had a connection with these children. He talked with them even though they couldn't speak English. On his first day walking to the school door, John waved me off happily as I stood there crying. After his first school day, we finally got back home.

'Mum, it's so good to be home and have a bit of peace and quiet,' he sighed.

These are words you'd expect from an old person, not from the mouth of a six-year-old.

Today, John is a strong Aboriginal man — strong in his identity and in his sexuality. When he was twenty-one, he told me that he wanted to share something with me.

'Mum, you have another daughter.'

I stared into his deep, brown eyes. 'What do you mean?'

'It's me, Mum. I'm gay.'

I wasn't shocked. My heart had known all along.

'Nothing has changed,' I reassured him. 'You're still our son and we will love you always. We're here to support you.'

Many times when John was younger, his dad had wanted to speak with me about this, but I wasn't ready. When John came out to me, I felt nothing but love for him. But I feared it would be a hard road ahead for him because, being black and gay, he would face many judgements. When he first told me, I also said, a bit selfishly, that I felt let down because that would mean I'd get no grandchildren from him.

Later, after seeing many of his drag shows, I asked him, 'Bub, did you really want to *be* a girl?'

'You should know, Mum. When you're on stage, you become a character. When I do a show, I dress and act as a diva. I don't want to physically become a girl. I'm happy with who I am.'

John is a brilliant performer. He's a tap dancer, Aboriginal dancer, singer and actor, and his dad and I are very proud of him.

Our daughter Lisa is shy, even today. She is very loving, and she made me realise that I was everything to somebody. She was a content baby, but she didn't like eating her food; she just wanted the bottle all the time. We had to throw it away when she was about four years old. She always clung to my skirt and cried if I left her. When Lisa was a toddler, she would say to me, 'I love you Mummy.' I would reply, 'I love you back.' Her bottom lip would drop and she would sadly say, 'But what about my front?' I would hug her and tell her that I loved her front and all of her.

Whereas me and John are outgoing and don't mind being out on stage, Lisa doesn't like the limelight. We took her to dancing, guitar, even martial arts, but she wasn't interested, so we didn't push her. Lisa did well at school, and she loves horses. Every Saturday, we took her to a farm where she could spend the day looking after them and ride in the afternoon. Today, Lisa is a wonderful mother; she is good with money, and her place is always spick and span. I am very proud of her. She has grown to be a beautiful young woman.

Jerry taught our children the Nyungar lingo. And he always sang to them,

Lock them out! Get them gone!
All the little rabbits in the fields of corn.
Envy, jealousy, malice and pride,
They must never in my heart abide.

Today, he sings these same songs to our grandchildren.

We played with our children a lot. Even if there was work to do, the children came first. Besides completing my hairdressing apprenticeship, I consider raising my kids well as my greatest achievement, because I never had a role model.

No matter where Jerry and I lived, Debbie visited us with her kids once a year. When Debbie got with her partner, they moved to Port Hedland, but we kept in touch. Then she moved to Darwin. She was up there when Cyclone Tracy hit on Christmas Eve, 1974. That evening, while having tea, this overwhelming feeling hit me and I wept.

'What's the matter?' Jerry asked.

I didn't know, just had a feeling that something bad was happening with my sister and I couldn't stop crying. Then we heard what had happened. A cyclone had devastated Darwin. It was totally wiped out.

That Christmas week, we were visiting Jerry's parents in Brookton.

'We have to go home,' I warned Jerry. 'We have to go home now.'

'All right, let's go.'

As we pulled into our driveway, Debbie pulled up in a taxi behind us. They had been evacuated.

'Yeah, we were expecting you,' I said.

Debbie and me have a telepathic connection. We've always had it. She told me that while the storm was happening, she was thinking that she might never see me again. She told me how she wrapped her body around her little son, shielding him with her back to the bathroom wall. Water came in through the floor, and her ears popped from the howling wind. Even today, she is scared of the wind.

In 1975, Debbie was turning twenty-one. I bought gifts for her throughout the year. For my twenty-first, I didn't get anything, so I wanted to make it special for her.

A whole boxful of gifts was sent off to the Derby Post Office. None of us had phones in those days, and apparently that box stayed there for nearly three months until one day Debbie was walking past the post office and had a feeling she should go inside.

'Anything for me?' Debbie asked.

'Yes, it's been sitting here for months!' the clerk said.

Debbie is very special to me. Music and singing are a big part of us. Debbie loves Slim Dusty's music and, when we're together, I've always got my guitar. We end up singing hymns too because that's what we grew up with. We are so close because we share the same past, which still affects us both today.

Until 2015 Debbie lived with her son in Djarindjin Aboriginal Community, north-west of Derby. That year, the state government was talking about closing many remote Aboriginal communities, including Djarindjin, and removing our people from their Country in Western

Australia.[1] My family's water and power were being turned off. Their basic human rights were being taken away.

When Debbie lived in a different remote community — they've closed that one too — she became the Community Development Officer because they saw she had some education. She baked bread, worked in the kitchen and took care of the elders.

One day, Debbie brought a group of elders into town for shopping. They speak their language every day, but, when they come into contact with white people, they speak English. They walked into this shop, and one elder went up to the counter.

'Can I help you?' the shopkeeper asked.

The elder replied, 'I want 'im plour dat gid up 'imsulf.'

The shopkeeper turned to Deb. 'What does he want?'

'He's asking for that flour that get up himself,' Debbie laughed. 'Self-raising flour!'

Another time, they all went to the pictures where the blackfullas still have to sit right up the front. Debbie sat with the elders. When they were leaving, someone in the group threw an empty Coke can and it missed the bin.

The police immediately arrested Debbie for littering. In the cell, the cops tormented her and pulled her hair. One officer picked her up by the throat and pushed her against the wall. Debbie made a formal complaint.

On the day of the hearing, a few community people stood up as witnesses for Debbie. One by one, as they came in to say what they saw happen, they placed their hands on the Bible.

The white man up front said, 'Can you swear on the Bible—'

Before he could finish the sentence, they each let full rip with every swear word you can think of. That's what they thought they had to do. The court was in uproar. Deb had to tell them it meant that in this court they just must tell the truth on that book.

7

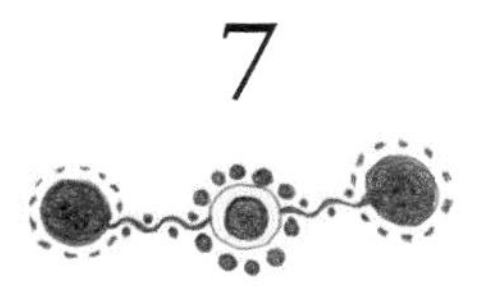

Death in custody

One night at home, early in 1983, Jerry made an announcement.

'I'm thinking about putting in for a position to run a cop shop. What do you think?'

'Go for it!' I replied.

So he did.

He put in his application and we were surprised when he was offered the job of running a police station. We didn't think they would let a blackfulla be the boss. We were thrilled. He was given the position of Senior Sergeant-in-Charge at Perenjori police station.[1] Only Jerry and a traffic cop would be employed there. In this position, Jerry'd wear five hats: policeman, clerk of courts, prosecutor, bailiff for the local court and sheriff for the Supreme Court.

We packed up our house in Perth, put it on the rental market and off we went to start this new adventure. After a full day's drive north, we arrived and moved into the police family house, next door to the police station. The station was old and the prison section built of tin. Next morning, three farmers arrived to check Jerry out. It was like a cowboy movie when the local gunslingers come in to sort out a problem.

We really liked it and ended up spending three years there. Nobody wanted us to leave. Jerry was well respected in both the black and white communities, and had a major impact on the Aboriginal community. He helped a lot of our people who were frightened of police as, historically, they had been the kidnappers and oppressors.

Jerry tested our people and approved their drivers' licences. Many were driving without licences. After Jerry had put through a hundred or more, the head office in Perth began to wonder why the numbers were so high. Usually, it was because officers were taking a payment to pass people. In Jerry's case, however, it was because the locals trusted him as one of their own.

My jobs included cleaning the police station, cooking for prisoners and working as the local hairdresser. The old police home was real beautiful with fireplaces in every room and a toilet out back. The whole neighbourhood could hear little Johnny singing in the toilet.

The prison was a shed basically — hot in summer and freezing in winter. But the prisoners ate whatever we ate. On Sundays, they had bacon and eggs with tomatoes and toast because that's what we always had. None of them ever wanted to leave. They would offer to mow our lawn or cut our wood, if we would let them stay.

Quite often Jerry had to go out to cover the whole area. One day, while he was away on his police rounds, a car pulled up. I looked out the window to see a policeman from Morawa. He paced around his police car, over and over again. What's wrong with this fulla? I thought, and walked to the back door.

'Excuse me, mate. You okay?'

'Can you tell me where Jerry is, please?' the officer asked.

'He's out on a job. Want me to give him a message?'

He paused and exhaled. 'Can you tell Jerry to tell all the blackfullas from this town to stay here to have their drinks and fights and not come to *my* town and give me headaches!'

Whenever female prisoners came in, it was my job to search them. One day, Jerry told me he'd brought in an Aboriginal prisoner. He asked me to come and search her. I refused.

'But this is your role,' Jerry insisted. 'I'm in charge of the police station and you have to search the female prisoners.'

So I went. When we got there, he opened the doors. No one was there.

'Where is she?' I asked.

There was a long silence.

'Ta-da!' With smiling faces, out jumped our two children.

Tears burst out of me. I'd been dreading having to search an Aboriginal woman.

'Don't ever do that to me again,' I sobbed.

The family thought it would be a good joke. They all came and gave me a big hug.

One time, when Jerry was driving back from a job, he ran over a goanna.

'Look what we've got for tea!' he said, holding out his prize by the tail.

Into a roasting tray it went and into the oven.

Then we got a call from a farmer for help. We all drove out to the farm. Jerry attended to the police business while we enjoyed scones and tea from flash teacups and saucers.

When we got back home, smoke was billowing out of our kitchen.

'Bulay! Ulliwah! Look here! The goanna's as hard as a rock!'

I carried the tray to the back door.

Suddenly, this white face appeared through the flyscreen.

'Can you tell me where the local policeman is?' the white man asked.

'Yes, you've come to the right place,' I replied.

'No, no,' he shrugged. 'I need to find the policeman, right now.'

'Yes, yes, you're at the right house.' I stood in front of him with a burnt goanna on a baking tray, its claws and tongue still hanging off it. 'I've burnt our dinner I reckon.'

The look on his face was priceless. I don't think he could believe an Aboriginal family was running the police station.

We chucked the burnt goanna to our chooks, but even they turned their beaks up at it.

In all our time in Perenjori, Jerry never locked up one Aboriginal person. People held Jerry with such great respect that they didn't cause any trouble. When people paid their fines, Jerry sent the amounts off to the Treasury and the Police Head Office. When we had police inspections, every cent was accounted for. On these visits, I felt uncomfortable because I never let white people into my house before, and I hated giving the officials tea, coffee and scones, but this was expected of me. We had a good time at Perenjori. It was the place and time I remember being happiest in my life, and I didn't want to leave.

One summer night in December 1983, Jerry and the kids were sleeping. It was around midnight, but I sat wide awake, reading some magazines in the dining room. One article was about Father's Day. It had pictures of children with their fathers. I started to cry, thinking that one day I'd like to meet my father. Everything was quiet and here I was alone, thinking that I'd like to meet and get to know him.

A nice, long bath comforted me. The warm water rose, and I jumped in up to my neck, relaxed, and let my mind think about my father. Then I went to bed.

Very early the next morning, the phone rang. A relation from Carnarvon was calling to tell me that my father had passed away.

When he died, my father was in Broome prison, doing time for running over two people. The cops say he was drunk. He got four years, but could get parole.

My father, Ronald Mack Ugle, was born on 17 August — the same date as my birthday — in 1930 in scrub at Tamala Station, close to Shark Bay, in Nhanda Country of the Gascoyne region. In 2010, when I was studying at Griffith University in Brisbane, I wrote to Freedom of Information (FOI) in the Department of Child Protection in Western Australia, asking for more information about him.

Teens Cottage residents, 1964. Front row from left: Lynda James, Cora Maron, Rhonda, Bunda (Eileen McKenna), and Trudy Hayes. Back row from left: Peter Coppin, Lester Drummond, Michael Hughes and Don Ard.

Granny Ruby Beasley (born Spratt) who worked in the mission laundry.

Top: Picnic at Miaboolya Beach, circa 1963. Rhonda is in the back row, far left; Marine James stands third from left. In the front row, second from left, kneels Rhonda's sister Debbie; third from right sits Beverley Pickett, then Susan Samson; and finally Marjorie Hughes kneels far right.

Left: Rhonda's mother, Alice Ethel Spratt (married name Webb), at Rhonda's wedding in Wembley, Perth, 1972. 'She loved green, so that outfit is green.'

Left: Rhonda's great-grandmother on her mother's side, Nellie Male (married name Spratt), was forcibly sent to Moore River Native Settlement, as were all of her children (including Rhonda's grandfather, Clarrie). This photo was given to Rhonda by Nellie's son, Jack. 'People always said that both my mother and I looked like Nellie.'

Below: Nana Edna Ronan (far left) with her mother Alice Ethel Ronan (born Robinson), and the rest of her family. Nana Edna named her own daughter Alice, after her mother.

Rhonda and Jerry's wedding at Wembley Church of Christ, Perth, 8 January 1972.

All the girls ready for Sunday church. Front row from left: Rhonda, Roslyn Flanagan, Beverley Pickett, Susan Samson, Bunda, Anna Hayes, and Marjorie Hughes. Lynda James stands behind Marjorie.

Loading up the truck with wood. Rhonda stands atop the woodpile, left of Marine James.

Swimming at Shelly Beach. Front-left eating watermelon is Laurie Tittum. Front-right eating watermelon is Peter Coppin.

Left: Second from left is Rhonda's father, Ronald Mack Ugle. Right of him stands his mother, Sylvia. His death in custody in Broome in 1983 was a trial case in the National Royal Commission into Aboriginal Deaths in Custody in 1990. Right: Rhonda and her sister Debbie when they were 'inmates' at Carnarvon Native Mission. They are wearing shoes for church on Sunday.

Rhonda at the Gascoyne River in 2007.

Rhonda with Elder, Uncle Albert Holt, and Brisbane Lord Mayor, Graham Quirk, honouring National Sorry Day in 2014. The three candles represent truth, justice and healing.

Rhonda with then Prime Minister, Kevin Rudd, on National Sorry Day 2011, three years after the official apology.

Carnarvon reunion, 2007. From left: Aunty May Foley, Irene Tittum, Rhonda, Tommy Jones and Roslyn Flanagan.

At Karatha, on the way to the 2013 mission reunion. From left: Lynda James, Beverley Pickett, Kathy Ryan, Rhonda, and Betty Kelly.

Brolga Dreaming, *1994. Rhonda's first painting.*

Child of the land, *2013. She is in harmony with the natural world. She lives life in the old ways — life before Captain Cook. Her spirit comes alive in me. She comes to me at night and I can feel her presence. All natural things are her family: the animals, trees, rocks, the sea, the river, the flowers. The sugar-glider is her totem. Her totem is her spiritual guide. Her totem brings her messages, and she must not harm it or eat it. It must be honoured and respected always.*

Dancing goannas, 2013. *After the rains, the creeks and billabongs fill with water. The land is lush with plenty of food for birds and animals. Goannas are like our bread because they are always there, whatever the season. So, I like to honour goannas by drawing them. I feel that, without them, we may not have survived. They were our staple food in times of plenty and in times of drought.*

Rainbow snake dancer, *2014*.

I found out that my father had grown up on Dirk Hartog Island where his father, Henry Ugle, worked as a stockman. My Grandfather Henry died young of a heart attack. He was just thirty-four, and my father was only eleven years old. Native Affairs had wanted to take the children away to the Moore River Native Settlement, but my grandmother, Sylvia, took the family to Carnarvon. She got a job in a pub, to keep her kids with her.

When my father finished school, he worked on different stations around Carnarvon. He was a gun shearer and a top stockman. In 1959, he became an Australian citizen. It made me sad to know that gaining his citizenship meant he had to turn his back on being an Aboriginal person, and he couldn't mix with his own mob, including me.

Community Welfare records say he was a heavy drinker, making him violent, but he always seemed to keep his job. The last position he had was for the Carnarvon Shire Council as a gardener. My mission friends often show me the trees around town that my father planted and say what a good worker he was.

About ten years after my father died, I was at the Aboriginal Medical Centre in Ipswich. They had all the reports there on black deaths in custody. Each person had their own book. I just happened to go up and check it out, and saw my father's name. For a long time, I couldn't open it. I thought about it, but it's only been in the last couple of years that I googled his name again.

My father first got picked up by the cops when he was eighteen. The charge against him was disorderly conduct. From then until 1982, he was in trouble a few times for minor things. But in November 1982, he got convicted of drink driving and manslaughter. Judge Hammond of the Carnarvon District Court said:

> *You have not accumulated any vast record of prior convictions. It is also clear that a very great number of people speak very highly of you and of your work and of your place in the community. The fact is, however, that on this day in May of 1982 you drove*

> *a vehicle when you were grossly affected by alcohol...these offences do really come within the more serious...because of the state you were in at the time and the total lack of fault on the part of the two people who were killed.*[2]

My father was just fifty-three and in prison when he died of a heart attack on 12 December 1983. Documents I've obtained say that 'medical records have gone astray in the prison system, and it could not be established what medical examinations, if any, Ugle had received in custody'.[3] He was on no medication, and they had no written records showing heart trouble. The medical records only showed injuries and sickness from drinking grog.

Seven years after my father passed away, they held an inquiry into his death. It was part of the Royal Commission into Aboriginal Deaths in Custody (1987–91). This national inquiry came about because of the high number of deaths among Aboriginal people being held in custody, in prisons and lockups, in Western Australia and Queensland in the 1980s.[4] Although, in the end, they decided that his death was because of a heart attack, in the submission my father's death was said to be 'caused or contributed to by injuries suffered while in prison'.[5]

The inquest found that several days before he died, my father asked if he could go to his brother's funeral.[6] Permission was refused. My father's cellmate, my mission brother Laurie Tittum, told the court that my father was very quiet and sad in the days after that. My father died on the day of his brother's funeral. Maybe, in part, he died from a broken heart, unable to say his final goodbyes.

The day before he died, my father's wife visited him in prison. She said he was okay, and that she had no worries about him.

In the report of the Inquiry, this is how they described the day of my father's death:[7]

> *Early in the afternoon of the following day Ugle and his cell-mate attended a work parade in the prison. They then returned to their cell.*

Ugle lay down and the cell-mate observed him to be breathing heavily and making what he considered to be funny noises. He ran to the gatehouse and informed a prison officer that Ugle was in a bad way. The prison officer immediately went to the cell and found Ugle breathing loudly, seemingly short of breath and in a semi-conscious state. With the other prisoner he took the mattress off the top bunk of the cell and started the ceiling fan. A senior prison officer then arrived. It was decided to take Ugle to hospital in a prison vehicle rather than wait to summon an ambulance. The hospital was a short distance away.

As soon as prison staff were notified that Ugle was ill, they took prompt action in assessing his condition and immediately transferring him to the Broome District Hospital. No criticism was made in relation to the actions of the prison officers confronted with this crisis, nor was there any room for such criticism.

Three officers placed Ugle in the rear of the escort wagon. He complained of pain in the chest, and was breathing heavily. At 1.15 pm he was taken to the Broome District Hospital. During the trip to hospital he remained conscious, was seen to be perspiring heavily, and to be having trouble breathing.

[The Doctor] attended Ugle in the emergency room of the hospital. He took a brief history from Ugle who complained of pain in the chest radiating down both arms, and noted that he had not previously been admitted to hospital with a heart attack.

[The Doctor] observed the prisoner to be conscious but not alert, breathing rapidly and having cold sweaty skin.

As he commenced administering intravenous pain-killers, Ugle's heart stopped...[The Doctor] attempted resuscitation... Another doctor assisted by placing a tube in his throat. They continued to attempt resuscitation for fifteen minutes but were unsuccessful in obtaining a pulse.

At 1.55 pm it was noted that Ugle's pupils were fixed and dilated. Attempts at resuscitation were discontinued at 2.25 pm.

The inquiry found that, at Broome hospital, my father was given 'prompt and appropriate treatment by medical staff, and that, while they tried hard to resuscitate him, they were unsuccessful'. A heart specialist said that there was nothing in my father's medical history to suggest heart disease. If they had looked deeper, they would have found that his father had died of a heart attack at a young age. In the end, the inquiry found that my father's death was 'due to acute congestive cardiac failure due to coronary heart disease; and...natural causes'.[8]

My mission brother, Laurie Tittum, remembers my father well.

'I used to ask him to tell me some yarns about the old days,' Laurie recalls. 'He would tell me about Shark Bay. He was a good storyteller. He was a boxer, a rodeo rider, and a horse breaker. He worked on the fascine in Carnarvon too. All of the palm trees along the fascine he planted. He was a very busy man. A solid man. When you sit down and talk to a man like that, you gain a lot of respect.'

'But he was a very hard man too,' Laurie goes on. 'Strong. Well, I thought he was anyway. He liked his rollies, his Log Cabins. I couldn't even cadge a smoke off him, that's how tough he was. He would put people in their place straightaway. And he never asked me. He never took advantage of anyone.'

This is how Laurie remembers what happened the day my father died:

> *Ron came back in from his washing job in the prison laundry. I was sitting back, reading. I asked him if he could spin me a yarn. But he lay down on his bunk, and he started breathing heavy.*
>
> *His eyes was rolling around in his head, and I knew something was wrong. I told the screws to get down here quick. They ran from the office up to the cell. We put the fans on, trying to get a bit of fresh air 'cause it was summer and very hot. But we couldn't bring him 'round.*

But they didn't call him an ambulance. They put him in the back of the escort van. Bloomin' hot too. They were standing in the car bay with him in the hot car, and he was starving for breath. And it was a hot day. They put him in that hot wagon, and that's what knocked him around. No oxygen masks or nothing.

They took him to the hospital, but apparently it was too late.

Once he died, they didn't want me there. I stayed in the bottom cells, chatting with the other Yamatjis. That afternoon, I camped down in the cells with the other fullas. I told the screws I was right to move back into Ronald's cell. When I went there that night, he was sitting there looking right at me, wanting to say goodbye.

Laurie said he thinks my father would have survived if they'd given him oxygen and put him in an ambulance, not left him untreated in the hot prison vehicle.

I believe my father's spirit called me that night as I lay in the bath, the day he died, as my thoughts went to him.

I needed to go to his funeral. The police wouldn't let Jerry off work on compassionate leave, so a friend and my kids came with me. We drove up to Carnarvon.

I decided to go to the viewing in the church. So my first look at my father was in his coffin. It was a hello and a goodbye at the same time. I kissed his forehead. Meeting him had been on my mind for a while, but I never thought I would meet him in death, or that the first and only touch from daughter to father would be a kiss to his cold forehead. We never shared a warm hug or a laugh. And I never heard his voice. With his death, all chance of this was gone. But from that day, I carried him in my heart.

On the day of the funeral, my friends and children came with me to the church. I didn't even know if the family knew who I was — that I was his daughter. I sat right up the back, feeling like an intruder.

I knew I had other brothers and sisters. My father had married and fathered another thirteen children. The family sat down the front. I sat up the back and sobbed and sobbed.

When they got up to read the eulogy, they read out all of his children's names. Then I heard my name read out. They had known all along. My new brothers and sisters really embraced me, and accepted me as their big sister.

My father's death affected me deeply. For a man I didn't know — for a father I'd never met — he touched me emotionally, filling me with sorrow.

Black man's law

Keys rattling
Doors slamming
Muffled voices
Footsteps echo down
Cold concrete corridors
Time forgotten, standing still
Like time has died

Hostile places, jail
Everything hard
Nothing soft
Crime committed
Time to do
White man's law, so untrue

Black man's law, no walls no time to do
Face your punishment like a man must
Black man's law true.

8

Terrorised

In 1991, when Jerry, me and the kids were all still in Perth, I was acting in a play called *Munjong*, written by Dr Richard Walley, an Aboriginal playwright, dancer and didgeridoo player.[1] The play is about the Aboriginal community's relationship with the police.[2] *Munjong* centres on a vengeful, redneck, white police constable who hates all blacks and decides to arrest Gunna, a roguish Aboriginal man, played in our production by acclaimed actor, Frank Nannup. My character was an Aboriginal activist.

The play also involves an Aboriginal woman (who is very fair and doesn't know that she is Aboriginal) who is the white policeman's wife. The policeman arrests Gunna who dies in custody under suspicious circumstances. As the play unfolds, his wife slowly realises that she is Aboriginal, and that the man who died in custody was her uncle.

I had always enjoyed the performing arts, but this was my first acting role. While rehearsing, *Munjong* brought up many issues for all the actors. The play related to our own lives. Many of our family members had died in custody, so this play reflected our reality — a reality that in some way touches every Aboriginal person. Many tears were shed.

After performing one evening, two cast members, Aaron Kearing and Frank, asked me to give them a lift. I agreed. Aaron asked me to drop him off at East Perth train station to meet his wife who was coming in from Kalgoorlie on the midnight train. When we pulled up at the carpark, it was not quite twelve. There was a taxi rank with one other car parked there. Because that car was there, I decided to park there too. Aaron got out to ask the station master what time the train would arrive.

Before he left, I asked him to give me his drink, a cider.

'Don't go walking around with your drink,' I said.

He passed it to me, I put it on the console and he walked off.

While we waited, Frank smoked out on the footpath. Aaron came back to say that the train was running a bit late.

We were enjoying each other's company until this lady walked past. She gave us a look of disgust — a real hateful look. We laughed it off, joking about her never seeing blackfullas before, and thought nothing more of it. We sat there talking, and Aaron told us about the time his family was terrorised by the police Tactical Response Group (TRG).

After a while, I asked Aaron to check again with the station master how late this train would be because I was getting tired. When he came back, a big white vehicle pulled up behind me with the headlights beaming. As Aaron walked towards the car, he turned and started heading in a different direction.

'Come on, Frank. Let's go see what Aaron's doing,' I said.

When we caught up with Aaron, he said he was all right now because his family was here.

'Well, your bag's in the car and your drink's here, so come and get your stuff,' I said.

He did. We waved him off and told him we'd see him at the theatre tomorrow.

Driving out, that big white vehicle still followed my car. We passed the taxi drivers who stood staring at us with serious faces. We made another joke about them never having seen black people before either. We didn't know that the lady who'd sat in the car in front of us had told them that she had seen me, the driver, hanging my arm out of the driver's window with a pistol in my hand. She'd told them that I was playing with the trigger. The taxi drivers had rung the police on their radio. That car following me was an unmarked troop carrier filled with TRG mob.

I noticed another car, further behind, driving very slowly.

'Why is that car going so slow? There's nothing blocking it,' I commented to Frank.

We passed the East Perth football grounds and continued on. Then we came to Wittenoom Street and a red light. I pulled up.

Next minute, all hell broke loose. Sirens wailed and lights flashed everywhere. Frank's face went dull with fear.

'It's okay, brother. It's just a breathalyser,' I reassured him. 'We'll be right 'cause I haven't been drinking.'

When the light turned green, I pulled over and waited for the fellow to come over to the window. We just sat there, talking. Next minute, this big voice bellowed through a megaphone.

'Can the driver of the car come out with your hands up!'

I looked to Frank.

'What the bloody hell's going on? Why do I have to get out with my hands up?'

I stayed there in shock, not moving. Then that voice through the speaker became wild.

'Can the fuckin' driver get out of the fuckin' car with your fuckin' hands up!'

By this time, fear gripped me. I opened the door and slowly put up my hands. All roads at the intersection were blocked with vehicles. One had swung in front of us, blocking our path ahead. When I stepped out onto the road, spotlights shone on me and guns pointed at me.

The men were dressed in black — their entire bodies covered — and their faces masked by balaclavas. They were screaming at me to get down and 'spread-eagle'. I'd never heard that term in my life. What did it mean? I sat cross-legged like a blackfulla in the middle of the road. That just made them real angry.

'Spread fuckin' eagle! Spread fuckin' eagle! We'll blow your fuckin' head off!'

I thought to myself that I had to lay down, but didn't know if it meant on your back or your tummy. I walked to the back of the car and lay face down on the road. My heart pounded against the earth and I feared for my life.

Because of my high heels and beautiful, feminine pink dress, maybe I didn't fit the image of a criminal, so they didn't search me. I lay still on the ground.

Then they shouted out for the passenger in the car to do the same. As soon as Frank got out of the car, they all rushed him. He was tall, dressed in black, with a beanie in our colours of black, yellow and red. Their feet ran fast over to him. Frank shouted and screamed out in pain. I turned to him.

'Are you all right, brother?'

I started to get up off the ground to go over to him. That's when one of them yelled, 'Put your fuckin' head down or we'll blow your fuckin' head off!'

The officer pumped the action on the gun.

I thought I was dead. What went through my mind at that moment was the thought of all of our people who had died at the hands of police. Would I become another black person that they just shot and murdered?

About a year earlier, police had gone to Marrickville in the inner west of Sydney and broken down a door where a husband lay sleeping in bed with his wife and two children. They shot the man dead in his bed. They later discovered that he wasn't the man they had wanted.[3] It was his brother they were after. An innocent man had been murdered.

Now, I tried to talk to the TRG cops.

'What's going on?' I asked.

'Shut the fuck up!' the policeman shouted.

Frank called out, 'Her husband's a policeman!'

I got cross with him. 'You shouldn't have said that, brother.'

But they let him up when he said that.

They searched my car, looking for guns.

'You won't find any guns in there,' I protested uselessly. 'Only my husband's golfing stuff, 'cause he loves golf.'

Then I suggested to one of them that he should come and see the play we were in.

'It's about you police and us Aboriginals.'

That officer replied, 'I know.'

My husband told me later that even when they arrested one of the most infamous Australian criminals, nicknamed the Postcard Bandit (Jerry had been there), the police had treated that criminal with more dignity and respect than they had treated me and Frank that night. *He* wasn't made to lay down spread-eagled on the road. And yet here was me, a person who had never broken any law, being treated like a dog.

When they let us up, they asked for our names and addresses. Anger and shock set in. Frank came over and gave me a hug. I asked for their names and numbers, and moved the covers off their numbers to write them down.

As we left, we shakily warned them, 'This isn't ending here. We're taking this further.'

'Nobody will care. You won't get nowhere,' the cops replied.

But that just fuelled a fire in me to take it as far as possible.

After the officers left, we got into the car to find they had filled it with rotting rubbish. They had emptied a stinking mess onto the seats. We slung it out onto the road.

After driving Frank home, I went on to my own home where Jerry was waiting for me. When he heard the story, he was furious. He went down to the payphone and rang the station, demanding to speak to the inspector. They said there wasn't one on duty.

'I know how the system works. Put him on please,' Jerry demanded.

While he was on hold, they sent some local police around to the phone box he was in and shone spotlights on him.

The next day, Jerry decided he wanted to resign. That day, while working in the law court, a message came over the loudspeaker.

'Sergeant Collard, you're wanted down in the prison cells,' the announcer said.

There were four sergeants in the centre, but Jerry was the main one for the detention centre. When trouble started, he was always the first one called. As soon as he heard his name, Jerry had this overwhelming feeling that he'd been set up. As he tried to stand, it was like he was stuck to the chair. He heard this almost audible voice saying, 'Don't go'. Jerry ignored the call, which was unusual. Eventually, one of the younger sergeants went down.

When Jerry finally got to the cells, he found out that the prisoner had attacked the young officer, breaking his jaw and knocking him unconscious. Six or eight officers were attacking the young white prisoner, strangling and punching him. Jerry had to pull them off to stop them from killing him. He got the feeling he was like a traitor for helping the prisoner.

He told me afterwards that it was like he got a warning from the spirits: 'Don't go down there.' He listened to that voice. It was a trap. They had wanted Jerry to get beaten up. Luckily, he listened to that voice of his ancestors. Jerry told me that if he'd gone down, he felt that prisoner would have killed him because the anger of that white fella was so great and Jerry's spirit and energy were so low after all of the years he'd spent speaking up for his people, and, recently, supporting me.

From that terrifying night on, the media set up on our front lawn. Strangely, the day before this incident, I had been proud to see Jerry on the front page of the *West Australian* as one of the longest-serving Aboriginal police officers in the state. He told about all of his good work with the community. The photo showed him standing there with his nephews, all in police uniforms. That had been a proud moment.

We had a lot of support from people, both black and white, through letters to newspapers, talkback radio, journalists' articles, and to us directly. The media announced that our play had 'come to life'. We even got a letter from the Police Commissioner apologising for the way Frank and me had been treated.

Rob Riley, then CEO of the West Australian Aboriginal Legal Service and a leading Aboriginal activist, told Jerry to stay in his job.

Aboriginal tells of police terror

By NORMAN AISBETT and JOHN DUFFY

THE shocked wife of an Aboriginal police sergeant was forced to lie spreadeagled on the ground after her car was intercepted by armed police in Lord Street, East Perth, early yesterday.

Rhonda Collard and Frank Nannup, a co-performer in a Perth play, had spotlights and guns trained on them by officers of the tactical response group and Division 79.

The incident happened after they had dropped another performer at the East Perth railway station.

It has outraged Mrs Collard and husband Gerry, a sergeant with 21 years' experience in the police force. His family has a long history of serving in the WA police force.

Sgt Collard tried to resign from the force in protest yesterday but a senior officer convinced him to take leave to consider his position.

Senior police later defended the actions of the officers involved.

Assistant Commissioner for operations Harry Riseborough said it was a proper and responsible approach to a report, from a member of the public, that someone in the vehicle might be armed.

The report proved to be groundless after Mrs Collard's car was stopped soon after midnight.

Mr Riseborough allowed the media to hear tape recordings of the alleged gun sighting being reported to the police communications centre and the conversations of officers at the scene.

He said a senior commissioned officer went to the Collards' home at 3.10am to receive any complaint but none was received. The offer remained open.

Sgt Collard said last night he would not encourage his wife to lodge an official complaint.

"What's the point?" he said. "I know that the officers involved will be exonerated and their actions will be found to have been justified."

He said there were some excellent and non-racist police officers.

"But I must now decide whether I want to continue to work with the odd one or two who spoil it for everyone else," he said.

Mrs Collard, an Aboriginal dancer-songwriter, is appearing in the Richard Walley play "Munjong" at the Hole in the Wall Theatre, Subiaco.

She said she was startled to hear sirens and have spotlights put on her car in Lord Street.

"They were all around us like a pack of feeding sharks," she said. "They ordered us to lie on the ground. They were shouting at us. It was really scary."

She said that while spreadeagled she tried to look at Mr Nannup but an officer swore at her. Another officer trained a pump-action shotgun at her.

The terror ended when Mr Nannup told the gun-toting police that they had stopped a fellow officer's car and wife.

Cheryl Strowger, 18, of Morley, said last night that she raised the alarm after another car parked near her own. A person's arm was hanging out of a window, holding a silver object that she believed to be a gun.

In a statement last night, State Theatre Company season co-ordinator Aarne Neeme expressed outrage at the police action.

Mr Walley said the incident was typical of the attitudes of certain sections of the police force towards Aborigines.

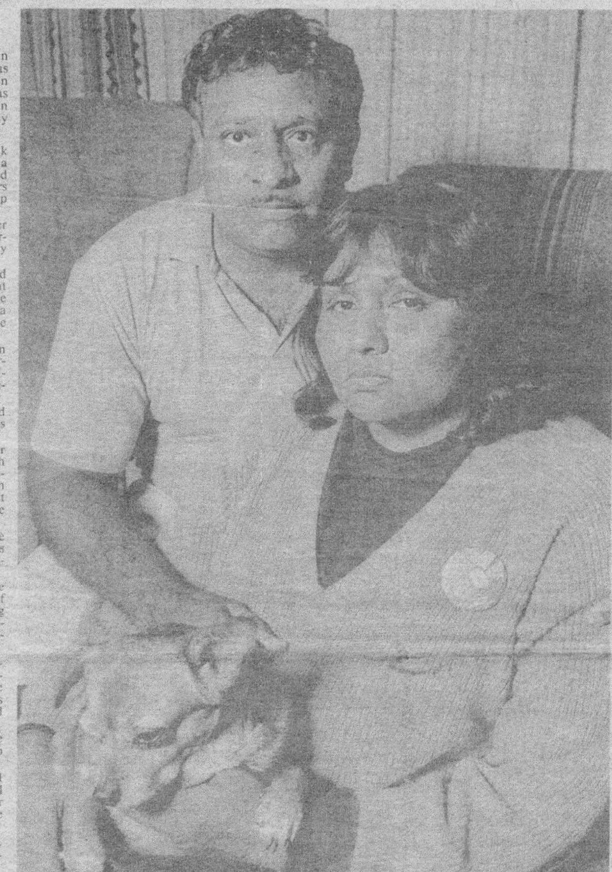

ANGRY: Sgt Gerry Collard and his wife Rhonda. Picture: RON D'RAINE

● **Editorial, page 10; Police advice, page 39**

'Aboriginal tells of police terror', The West Australian, *7 September 1991.*

NEWS RELEASE

From the office of the: W.A. LIBERAL LEADER

PR /91 SEPTEMBER 8, 1991 **COLLARDS TO BE COMPLEMENTED ON DIGNITY OVER ENCOUNTER**

Rhonda Collard and Frank Nannup are to be complemented on the dignified manner in which they are handling their unfortunate police encounter last Friday, Shadow Aboriginal Affairs Minister Richard Court said today.

"It is important that this matter is properly investigated as we can all learn from the mistakes made," Mr Court said.

"The police have an unenviable task in our community.

"But it is unfortunate that these two highly regarded citizens went through this trauma.

"The Collard family are great Western Australians and in addition to Rhonda's contribution to the arts her relatives have given years of unselfish service to the police force and other community services including alcohol and drug rehabilitation.

"Frank Nannup is an internationally acclaimed actor with his current performance in Munjong being brilliant.

"I only hope his humour shines through this regrettable incident."

Mr Court said he had discussed the incident with Shadow Police Minister George Cash who advised that in Parliament on Tuesday he would be calling on Police Minister Edwards to make a full statement on the matter.

News release by then WA Liberal leader and later WA Premier, Richard Court, 8 September, 1991.

In a newspaper article the day after the terror, Jerry, who'd been a police officer for twenty-one years by then, said that there was no point in us complaining to the police because he knew 'that the officers involved will be exonerated and their actions will be found to have been justified'.[4]

Jerry was right.

The police never said that they didn't stop my car, order me out at gunpoint and make me lie spread-eagled on Wittenoom Street,[5] but the police investigation found that:

> *Every police officer involved said there were no shotguns or obscene language, and 'vehemently denied that one police officer worked or pumped the action of a shotgun', and that this 'was completely unfounded'.*[6]

All of the officers involved also 'denied possessing knowledge that the occupants of the vehicle were Aboriginal'. While following my car, the police were told that it was registered to a Collard, a well-known Aboriginal name. And the witness, the woman who first told the taxi drivers that she thought I was hanging a gun out of my car, had 'walked past their car' at the train station to tell the taxi drivers.

The woman and the taxi drivers were looking back into our car from the front. I saw that she was white. She reckoned she clearly saw my finger on the trigger of a gun, but claimed she didn't notice that Frank and me were black.

Police tapes from their telephones and radios that night somehow got lost before the investigation. The report found that this was 'not satisfactorily explained by police'.[7] The investigation also decided that 'there was insufficient evidence to prove the complainant's allegations that excessive force was used'.

Our case got so much public interest and media attention that the Parliamentary Commissioner then did his own investigation.[8] By then, it was two years after that terrifying night.

Even though a witness said he 'saw a shotgun or other long-barrelled weapon produced by the passenger of the TRG vehicle', the

Commissioner was 'unable to come to any conclusions about the use of a shotgun'. He decided that 'the allegation that the action of the shotgun was pumped was unsubstantiated'. The Commissioner was also 'unable to determine whether obscene language was used by one police officer while Mrs Collard lay spread-eagled'.

Police officers testified differently about when the TRG arrived. Some said the TRG arrived after our car pulled up at the train station, and others said they were already parked a distance away and saw our car drive in. Did they send the unmarked TRG vehicle to follow us from the theatre after our show? It seemed strange to me that when I mentioned it to him that night, the officer knew what our play was about.

At our formal interview, Jerry told them that if we'd been white Australians they would not have made us lie on the ground, spread-eagled, at gunpoint.

The Commissioner's report decided that the police officers' actions were 'unreasonable', but there was 'no evidence to suggest that racial background had any bearing on the decision to involve high risk procedures'.

In the end, Frank and me were offered an 'act of grace' payment without accepting any liability by the police. We rejected it and they withdrew this offer. I didn't want their money; I wanted justice. Eventually though, we accepted a second offer.

Some of my lines from *Munjong* went:

> *During my childhood years I used to watch my relations get locked up in jail for a number of offences, which in those days we accepted as normal practice. Offences like being on the streets after six o'clock. Being in possession of alcohol. Travelling from one town to another without a permit. I ask you, brothers and sisters, have things got better?*[9]

The night after this event, we still had to put on the show. Richard Walley himself stood in for Frank, but I had no understudy. I had to pull myself together and perform. During one scene, where the police officer and I argue, in the script I'm only supposed to point my finger at him. But this night, I held my fist up to him. Richard thought I was going to actually punch him! But somehow I managed to get through the whole play without breaking down. We got a standing ovation and I burst into tears.

We left the stage and when we reached our dressing rooms, my son John was there waiting. We hugged and cried. He'd put a red rose into a beautiful little vase and, with my red lipstick, he'd written on the dressing-room mirror in big letters, 'Mum, be black, wise and strong.'

One day around this time, Jerry rang and asked me to pick him up from the law courts in the city after work. It was mid-winter. As I drove up, Jerry wasn't outside, but a group of white police officers stood there, talking. I freaked out. I didn't want them to see me. I combed my hair over my face, sweating with pure fear.

I drove slowly around the block. If he's not there, he can walk home, I thought. As I came around the corner, panic set in deep. Still no Jerry. Okay, last go. If he's not there this time, I'm going home. Luckily, this third time, Jerry was there.

A few weeks later at the law courts, Jerry wanted to make a cup of tea. He went to his locker to get his cup. Picking it up, he found that someone had used it as a toilet. When he saw his cup like that, he just dropped it to the floor and walked away from the police force forever. After all the years he'd been in the job, to be so disrespected and unsupported, this was the final straw.

Following that night, I began to isolate myself. For a time, my music stopped, and I couldn't sleep at night. People said I'd changed. I stopped doing my favourite things, like playing guitar and dancing. Since this incident, life's been really hard. I was always a positive person, but in the two years following this event, I never cried so much in my life. I feared that the phone was tapped, and that every car behind me was the police. I just wanted to get back to my old self.

Post-traumatic stress and depression from this event and others from my childhood are now a part of my everyday life. Even today, the sight of a blue light or sound of a siren turns my stomach. If I walk in the street and a policeman appears, I try to hide, so they can't see me. They make me sweat and shake. When you experience something like this, it turns your life upside down. It's only about two years ago that I finally got medical help from a local Aboriginal doctor.

Payback

With hidden identity
You hunt in packs
Like marauding dogs
You crave the kill

With tunnel vision
You stalk your prey
The black the poor the innocent

You turn your back on
Justice and humanity
They know you not

In your uniform of power and blue
In your white skin of privilege
You harass, torment, arrest, torture, kill
You hate my race and our Aboriginal skin

You are the jailers, jury, judge, executioner
The so-called law keepers…Ha! What a joke
Your actions scream louder than your words

We overflow your prisons
Yet we are two per cent of our land's population

My wish for you is after your death
You come back to this earth
Without your thin white skin
Wrapped up in a skin of black

Learn the painful force of your unjust laws
Feel the criminal act you lay on us
All in the name of your rich British queen
Everything you did will be done to you
The endless bashings, soul-cutting abuse
Petty charges, rapes, and murders

Have your spirit smashed and injured
Have no voice, trapped where life is lawless
Know deep despair, know fear and terror
Feel powerless, lost, invisible

All these feelings I wish for you
I freely give all these gifts
To have, to hold, forever and ever
Now in your new race, new face
Can you tell me how you feel
Walking in our shoes and Aboriginal skin?

9

The brolga and other stories from Mother

One day in 1993, the phone rang. Mother was asking to come and stay with me, Jerry and the kids in Perth. Me and her had spent the first three years of my life together, but it wasn't until now, as a middle-aged mother myself, that we lived together again.

During those three months, we sat down and talked one on one. She showed me how to do a bark painting. Instead of using paint, she glued on bark to show the brolgas, trees and other wildlife. While I watched, she told me the tale of the brolga she'd reared up on Gogo Station.

My mother loved fishing off the riverbanks. She'd got her love of fishing from her mother, Nana Edna. On the way back after fishing one day, she heard a little cheeping sound coming from the bushes. She looked down and found a baby brolga that had been abandoned. She picked up the little bird and brought it home.

Mother loved animals. Among her brood were bulldogs, roosters, chickens and cats. This little baby brolga joined the family of humans and animals. The cats and roosters gave the chick a good flogging. They didn't know that one day this bird would grow to be the tallest of them all. It even fossicked with its beak in the kids' hair for lice and nits. This brolga walked everywhere with the family. Wherever they went, it walked. It didn't know it had wings.

One day, Mother turned to my younger sisters and said, 'I think it's about time we taught this brolga how to fly.'

The family lived at the bottom of a tabletop hill. Up they walked, Mother, my sisters and the brolga. When they reached the top, Mother gently picked up the bird and threw it over the edge. Gracefully, it spread its wings and floated down to the bottom. When it landed, it looked back up to where its family was. Straight up, it walked all the way back up the hill to them.

'Maybe it needs a longer run up,' Mother suggested.

They all walked down to the dirt road. The girls took off flat out, with Mother running behind. She thought the bird would run to catch up with the young girls. But it didn't take off. It hung out with Mother, running beside her.

In the end, they gave up teaching the brolga to fly. Seasons came and went, dry and wet seasons. Then one day, Mother said that a flock of brolgas flew over and called out. The bird must have known its language. It was time for it to join its feathered family. It took off, in its own time, to join its own mob in the sky.

During this time, I asked Mother what our totem was. She said it was the curlew. In most Aboriginal mobs, curlews are a death bird, bringing messages of death. But in our family, she explained, only when it calls out three times is the curlew a messenger of sad news.

Mother also told me that the number three is special for our mob. When we dance, we must have three marks on our bodies. These marks represent our Dreaming spirit, our Guardian spirit, and our Mischievous spirit. It's amazing how I've always been drawn to odd numbers. Even before I knew about the special number three, I liked to paint animals and people in odd numbers like three or five.

While we were together, I asked Mother about her life. Her parents, Clarrie and Edna Spratt (born Ronan) had married in 1934 at Moore

River Native Settlement. That's the year Mother was born in Mullewa, inland from Geraldton, where Clarrie was droving cattle. She told me that when she was five both of her little brothers had died within two weeks of each other.[1] Nana Edna told her that all four children became sick together, so Nana took them to Carnarvon hospital where the two youngest died.

Nana was scared that she would lose the other two children if they stayed there, so she took them home with her. Mother and her older brother Harry survived. Two years later, her younger brother James, known as Jimmy but nicknamed Boogine, was born.

Nana's husband Clarrie was the son of my great-grandmother Nellie Male who'd been taken from the Kimberley to Moore River Native Settlement. Nellie, called a 'half-caste', married Jack Spratt, a 'full-blood'. Their son Clarrie grew up in Moore River, and this where he met Nana Edna.

Nana was one of seven children born to Alice Ethel Ronan (born Robinson). Nana named my mother after her own mother. In 1925, the same year that my grandfather Clarrie's mother, Nellie, was forcibly taken to Moore River, my grandmother Edna's mother, Alice, died there as the result of poor treatment. She was just thirty-one. Her children were two to twelve years old, including Nana who was ten.

A newspaper article, 'half-caste girl's death: A poignant deathbed document: Allegations concerning the Moore River Settlement which seem to call for some investigation', dated 5 September 1925, reported Alice's death.[2] It shows part of Alice's dying letter to her mother:

> *My Dear Mother, I am leaving this letter, I know that I won't see you. Mother, you know I am not telling lies. I would not die with lies on my lips. Mother, if you don't get this letter you will never know what's happened to me. I am trusting to God you will get this letter. He has given me strength to sit up and write this letter. What I can see of it they don't want you to see me alive because I would tell you a lot of*

> *things. —— —— is very cruel to me, saying I am only putting it on. I was told that I ought to be dragged out of bed and flogged and put in the 'boob'. Well, I can't help it, mother, they can do that. I've got no strength, even the —— —— came and said I was lucky to be there where I should be doing time in Fremantle. I killed nobody, mother, why should I be there. I am giving up hope...I suppose I've got to die here.*
>
> *...They gave me salts and caster oil...I couldn't help it. They handle me roughly and pulled me out of bed. I fell up against the wall and made a lump on my head. I asked them to send me to Perth, and they would not do it. I see nothing else for it but linger and die, unknown to you, do you see mother...Good-bye forever, from your dieing daughter.*

Letter to Mrs Robinson from her daughter, Alice Ronan (Rhonda's great-grandmother), as quoted in The Truth, ***5 September 1925.***

So Nana and her six brothers and sisters grew up without a mother at Moore River. As seventeen-year-olds, Clarrie and Nana ran away together. For that, Clarrie spent time locked up in Fremantle Gaol.[3] After that, Clarrie changed. He became cruel to Nana, and was often drunk. Even before Mother was born, Nana wanted a divorce. When Mother was a baby, the government moved the family back to Moore River.

When Mother was eight, her parents divorced, and Nana left the settlement to live with her new husband, Roy Bellotti. Children were not allowed to leave Moore River, so my mother and her two brothers grew up alone in that place without their parents. Nana Edna went on to have several more children.[4]

Mother told me of the cruelty at the settlement. Moore River was run by the government, not Christian missionaries. Officers shaved the children's heads and made them wear hessian bag dresses for punishment. For fighting in the dormitories, Mother often felt the pain of the strap.[5] Other punishments included the cane, fines and, worst of all, those who ran away or slept out at the Aboriginal camp spent days locked in scary cells known as 'the boob' — 'a prison within a prison'.[6]

I learned that my mother had a brave and adventurous spirit. She told me that when she was a young girl, she and two other girls ran away from the settlement with a married couple. The couple were Wongi desert people from Kalgoorlie way. They wanted to return to their Country. They had a greyhound, or 'kangaroo dog' as we call them. The group escaped in the dark and the old couple used the stars to map the way. When they reached the pipeline that goes from Perth to Kalgoorlie, they followed this as their guide.

Mother said they caught a kangaroo with their dog. While they were cutting its throat, Mother held its tail. They ate that kangaroo for food.

The police soon put out a warrant to arrest the group and bring Alice back to Moore River.[7] On their travels, the Wongi lady dressed Mother up in a hat, high heels and a pretty dress. Mother then knocked on farmhouse doors, offering a penny to buy eggs, bread or milk. Farmers never took the penny from the girl, they just gave her food. That's how they survived.

When they reached Merriden, half-way between Perth and Kalgoorlie, some Nyungar people told Mother that her father Clarrie was sick back in Moore River. Mother handed herself in to the police who sent her by train back to Perth. At just fourteen, Mother was held in the lockup there, waiting to be returned to the settlement.[8]

Months later she took off again, but was caught after a few weeks. Some time after that, the Superintendent at Moore River ordered Mother to start working, 'owing to the possibility of contamination by the bad element' at the settlement.[9]

Mother was sent to work as a domestic servant at the Coolart property in Walebing, a hundred kilometres away. She told me the missus there made her wear shoes to serve morning and afternoon teas. Mother had never worn shoes in her life. She tripped and fell, breaking cups and saucers and even their flash crystal.

'Breakages seemed to be the order of the day,' wrote the white lady in her complaint letter.[10]

Mother felt continuously growled at and eventually she ran away. She reported to the Moora police who took her to the Native Girls' Home in Perth. Two weeks later, in September 1949, Mother was sent by train to Yarrabubba Station in Meekatharra, over 700 kilometres north-east of Perth, to again work as a servant. This job didn't work out either, and six months later Mother was put back on a train for Perth.

Maybe she got the sack because her boss didn't want to increase her wage. It was up for review by the Commission of Native Affairs.[11] But her boss wrote, 'She is very tired in her work, and doesn't take any interest at all. On top of this she seems too fond of hanging around the men working here, and I don't feel like taking the responsibility of her.'[12]

Mother never arrived at the girls' home. Even though she was put on the train for Perth, she never reported in. She had taken off yet again. A handwritten note on the authorities' memo stated that the train fare would now be 'chargeable to Alice Spratt herself'.[13]

The police eventually caught up with Mother in Geraldton. She was still under the control of the *Native Administration Act (WA) 1936*. This meant that, like all Aboriginal children, she was controlled by the Chief Protector of Aborigines until she turned twenty-one. So Mother was breaking the white man's law by being on the run. She told them her next move was most likely to Carnarvon.

By September 1950, aged fifteen, Mother was working again, now on Mooroogue Station in Carnarvon, and giving 'satisfactory service'. This is where she met my father.

Ronald was four years older and, as she told me with her beautiful smile, 'tall, dark, and handsome'. Mother said they loved each other very much and that I was their love child. By early 1951, Mother was sixteen and pregnant. Ronald asked the government for permission to marry her. Mother needed her parents' approval too, but Nana Edna was against them being together and refused to sign the papers. So, as my aunty told me later, Mother signed the forms herself. The government approved Mother and Ronald's marriage, but they never got married. Seven months later, I was born in Carnarvon hospital.

Mother lived on The Block, on the fringes of East Carnarvon. She worked on stations nearby when she could. So that's where I lived for my first couple of years. I can remember horses around a big water tank, and me crawling towards an old Aboriginal woman sitting on the steps in the sun.

Before long, my mother got pregnant again. Not long after, she was asked to leave the family home. When she told me these stories, my father was not in the yarn. On 8 May 1954, my little sister, Debbie Ann Spratt, was born. We had moved by now to live in the sandhills at the back of the block. Here, our home was four sticks with a hessian bag for a roof. One of my aunties helped out by giving us food.

Exactly how Debbie and I were taken I don't know. Debbie said she asked Mother one time and was told that Native Welfare just came and took us one day. Documents say that we were admitted to Carnarvon Mission on 12 December 1954, but the names of who admitted us and why we were admitted have been deleted, and I never got to ask Mother myself.[14]

I have since learned that single Aboriginal mothers were especially likely to lose their children back then because most could not find work and, until the early 1960s, they could not get social security.[15]

My mother was nineteen when Debbie and me were taken, but even though she had two daughters, because she was under twenty-one she was still controlled as a 'child' under the Native Act. Mother and us girls were also assessed as 'half-castes' under the racist policies of the time, and so me and Debbie were more likely to be taken.

One day while she was painting, Mother ran out of bark. We went off into the bush together and collected different paper barks for her artwork. It was a beautiful day. I remember how special it was, having her to myself and being in her company. It reminded me of being a hunter-gatherer again — enjoying the sunshine, walking on the earth, taking bark, but thanking the trees for the bark as we went. Here I was out in Mother Nature with my own mother.

After three months, Mother got word that my brother Jim had suffered a heart attack. She had to leave me. She took that brolga painting she'd been working on with her. If I die and come back as another living thing, I would like to be a brolga, so I can fly and dance in memory of Mother.

10

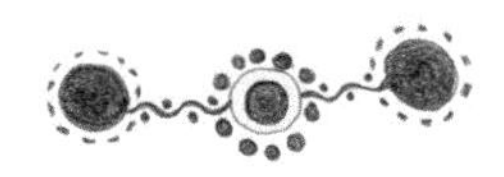

Sorry business

In 1993, the Year of the World's Indigenous Peoples, people were coming from all over the globe for a conference in Wollongong, south of Sydney. Having never left Western Australia, I was keen to go. At Perth airport, many other Aboriginal delegates gathered. The plane was a jumbo jet — the first I'd been on.

After arriving, unpacking and settling in, we chose which conference sessions interested us. The groups I can remember were the elders or youth. I chose to join the elders' group because I wanted to be around Indigenous elders from all over the world.

The delegates raised many issues. High on the agenda were land rights, health, education, identity, culture and keeping our languages strong. It was wonderful to hear the wisdom and insights of so many elders.

The Australian Aboriginal elders discussed having a national Aboriginal language, which could be taught and spoken all around Australia, similar to the Māori language of New Zealand. After long talks though, we reached no conclusion because of the number of Aboriginal languages. How could any one of these be shared across the whole nation when each one is connected to different tribal lands, sacred ceremonies, song lines, dances and Dreaming stories?

Elder

You sat on the earth
cross-legged and silent
Your silver hair soft and wavy
framed your beautiful dark face

Your expression spoke of sadness
as tears fell from your eyes
I could feel your confusion
and I could touch your pain

You see our young people
turn away from our ancestral ways
As time moves on passing through
they embrace all that is new
And all the new things it will bring

I will keep and hold our culture
Share with me our sacred laws,
stories, songs and dances
I will keep and pass them on forever

I need to hear our Dreaming stories
I need to hear our ancient songs
I need to dance our corroboree dances

I promise I will honour and respect our culture
and all that you teach me
With a strong heart and true spirit
I need our Dreaming
I need your wisdom
I need your knowledge
Oh, spiritual elders of our motherland.

At the elders' forum, I met Valentine Brown. My role was taking the microphone to the different speakers around the large hall and I happened to sit next to him.

'Hello,' I whispered. 'Where you from, brother?'

'Ipswich,' he replied.

This made me giggle because the name sounded very funny to me. From that first meeting, we had an instant attraction.

During later conversations, we found out that we both loved music. Val is a drummer and a singer, and I write songs, play guitar and love to sing. Our attraction for each other was so strong that we ended up having a one-night stand.

Our affair soon became all consuming. For many months, it continued by phone and letters between Western Australia and Queensland. I was obsessed and completely soaked in this drug called love. It blinded me, clouded my thinking, controlled my life. My common sense left me, just disappeared.

This affair came to light when my husband opened our phone bill and saw that it was very high. Jerry questioned me on who I'd been calling. He noticed the same number repeated over and over. Although I tried to deny everything, Jerry soon found a letter addressed to Valentine. The truth was out. Arguments erupted and tears flowed. We shouted many hurtful words at each other, which cut to the bone. Our lives ran out of control and turned upside down, all because of me.

This is very hard to write about because I know how deeply I wounded my husband and my beautiful daughter. I broke their hearts into a thousand pieces, which will take forever to mend. I have learned that family love is precious. It lasts forever. I have also now learned that some romantic love lives for a while then dies, fading away like an echo.

One morning, my husband packed my suitcase, drove me to work and angrily tossed my suitcase out onto the ground. My clothes scattered everywhere. I'd been kicked out of our home. With a heavy heart, I gathered up my belongings and then watched as my husband and daughter drove away from my life, but not away from my heart.

Not knowing where I would sleep that night, I asked my niece if I could stay with her until my life was sorted out. After a week, Valentine invited me to come live with him in Ipswich.

So, in 1994, I flew to Queensland. Over twenty years later, I'm still here. Many things have changed during these years. Valentine and me are no longer together. We split up in 2007, but remain good friends.

I needed to ask my family for their forgiveness because of all the hurt and pain I'd put them through. About five years after moving to Queensland, on a visit back home to Western Australia, I asked to talk to them both, my husband, Jerry, and our daughter, Lisa. We three sat down together.

'I need to say sorry to you both for leaving, and for all the pain and sadness I've caused.' My head bent down low. 'Could you find it in your hearts to ever forgive me?'

'Mum, I forgave you a long time ago,' Jerry replied straight up.

Lisa's face was full of tears.

I turned to her. 'I'm so sorry, bub.' We hugged.

Family

Girl-child sleeping on couch
Black and white picture on TV
Husband working nightshift
Man-child out on the town.
Dripping water in the sink
No Smoking signs everywhere.
Crickets sing their night songs
Images stare from the wall
The hands of time never still.
Light shines from the kitchen
The night quiet and still.

In 1996, Uncle Wodgee, one of mother's younger brothers, called me from Perth. Mother was sick. He told me I'd better get over there as soon as possible.

I was a day too late. Mother died before I even left Brisbane. Flying from Brisbane to Perth, I imagined her sitting on the clouds, smiling at me. My family came together at this time, and we yarned all evening on family history.

Mother was sixty-one when she died from undiagnosed leukaemia. A blood test in Fremantle hospital picked it up too late. It wasn't till after the funeral that one of my sisters told me that, in her final hours, Mother had kept asking for me, her first-born.

We needed to head from Perth to Derby for the funeral. From Perth we all flew up to Broome, and then me, Margie and Debbie with my nieces and nephews drove the rest of the way. It was late in the afternoon when we set out and, as me and my family were driving north, we saw frill-necked lizards running flat out on their two back legs, crossing the road. My sister Margie said they were a sign of good luck, in the Aboriginal way. While we travelled, I taught the kids some songs, and told stories.

The blue sky turned black. Heavy rain started to fall, and lightning raced across the sky. At sundown, we finally reached the town of Derby where my mother would be laid to rest.

I needed to go to the viewing to see her one more time, and say my final goodbyes. Lying there, she looked at peace, and as beautiful as I remembered her. It was like she was just in a deep sleep.

The morning of the funeral was sunny and warm. We all wore white and black, traditional funeral colours. At the service in the Catholic church downtown, the family took part, reading special verses from the Bible. I felt numb and couldn't cry, even though I wanted to. It was like my mind couldn't accept that I'd spent so much time looking for her, longing for her, and now I wouldn't see her anymore. That journey had come to an abrupt end.

We had spent some time together, but it wasn't enough to develop a close mother–daughter bond. I know that we are connected through blood, our looks, and I believe even spiritually — even now she comes to me in dreams — but as a mother and daughter we never rebuilt those ties because we had lived our lives separated by time and distance.

At the church, mother's sister, Aunty Carmel, handed me a card. It was to both me and Debbie, our only sympathy card. It said Mother was in the next room, and that she had just gone to sleep. That card meant a lot to me, and it is still with me today. It showed that Aunty loved us, and thought and cared about me and Deb on the loss of our mother.

What struck me at the graveside was that the earth was a rich, deep red. Debbie's son told me after, that as we stood there, he looked down and saw a little green frog, bright green against the red earth. Tooda said he thought that was a sign from Nana. Debbie and me were going to sing a hymn, but in the end we couldn't.

A couple of days later, we all jumped in the 4WDs, and headed out one last time to Gogo Station, to the house where Mother and my stepfather had lived. Everything was empty, and no one was around. Even the camps were deserted. We wandered through the abandoned house. No smell of cooking bread, no bully beef boiling on the stove, no barking dogs or scratching chooks. It was just an empty shell now, this house. We wandered through there, talking about memories.

On the journey back to Derby, my stepfather asked us to help him look out for cattle on the road. We forgot. Next thing, we nearly ploughed into a herd of them. We stopped just in time. As the cattle slowly moved off the road, in the middle stood a curlew, looking straight at us. Normally, they are very shy and run from cars and people.

'That's a sign from Mum,' I said. 'We'll be safe now.'

Sure enough, from then on we were fine, and no more cattle crossed the road.

I realised later that this was the first time I had called my mother 'Mum'.

We stayed at my youngest sister Janny's house. My stepfather Stan sat in the lounge room. As I walked past him, he caught my wrist.

'Rhonda, why don't you talk to me?'

I hadn't realised it until then, but we had never ever chatted in my life. Stan had been head of the house in the old-fashioned way. Maybe I felt I couldn't talk to him until now. I sat down next to him and we started to talk. He told me that, out of all the children, I looked most like my mother.

That afternoon we all sat on the veranda, playing cards, sharing a barbecue, and singing along to my guitar. Then Debbie said, 'Hey sis, let's sing "Yowie, My Brown Skin Baby, They Take 'im Away".'[1]

I strummed the guitar, and everyone joined in. Singing that song, we all started crying, even my stepfather.

I looked at him. 'I think it's time we talked.'

My sister Margie, my stepfather and me went into a side room. I told him about being ten years old, and receiving that Christmas letter from Mother. How happy it had made me. I told him how I memorised the address, and how I had then written every week to her — every week for six years. And I told him of my heartbreak at never getting a reply. All this time, I had hated my stepfather for not passing on those letters to Mother. Here I was now, myself a mother, a grandmother, forty-four years old, crying my heart out and saying to the white man, 'Dad, I think it's time we talked.'

We were all very emotional.

'Dad, I forgive you,' I said, 'but there's one thing I need to know. Did you take all the letters that I wrote to my mother and destroy them?'

I watched as tears fell from his pale blue eyes. Then he said, a little overcome, that they had never received any letters from me. All my years of hating this man for taking my letters, for taking Mother away from us, for being in the mission, I had laid the blame right at his feet. All this anger and hate that I'd carried in my heart for this man for all those years melted away in a flood of tears.

We stayed talking for some time. Talking and forgiving. I'd been lost in my own pain and had been blind to his. He shared stories about how, through the years, his white friends had told him to tell others that Mother wasn't Aboriginal, but that she was Indian. Or how he was invited to white families' homesteads for dinner, but was told to leave his Aboriginal wife at home, or for him to come alone. Or they'd say, 'Bring her along, but tell her she can't swim in the pool.' He would then turn them down. There were lots of stories like this that he told me.

Many years later, while reading government documents from my family's history, I learned even more.

In August 1958, when I was seven, my stepfather applied for a maternity allowance for Mother for their two sons. My mother was assessed as having 'a preponderance of 1/16 of native blood'.[2] This meant she was a 9/16 caste (just more than a half-caste). She was too black, and so wasn't allowed to receive a maternity allowance unless she became an Australian citizen.

Mother's maternity allowance and citizenship applications do not mention Debbie and me. We were left out. Debbie told me later that Mother was warned never to see us or speak with us, her two oldest daughters, ever again. This was part of 'dissolving native and tribal association', which was a condition of citizenship.[3] My mother was forced to turn her back on her Aboriginal family and culture.

714/48 90

D.N.W.
Inwards
28 OCT 1958

DEPARTMENT OF NATIVE WELFARE
OCT 1958
DISTRICT OFFICE, DERBY

DEPARTMENT OF NATIVE WELFARE

Report on Applicant for Certificate of Citizenship

Full name of Applicant: Alice Ethel WEBB

Date of Birth: 29/11/35 Caste: 9/16ths

Parentage – Father's Name: Clarence SPRATT Caste: 3/4

Mother's Name: Edna May BELOTTI Caste: 3/8ths

If married give date and place of marriage (legal) (tribal): 18/4/56 Fremantle WA

If married give name and caste of spouse: Stanley James Webb (Whiteman)

Give names and dates of birth of the children of applicant:
James Terrance 14/3/56
Richard George 9/5/58

Do these children live with the applicant? YES

If not, where are they? N/A

Do they attend school, and where? N/A

Does the applicant intend having children's names endorsed on certificate? YES If not, why? N/A

Is the applicant caring for any other children? NO

Are they maintained by the applicant? YES

How does the applicant earn a living and what wage is earned?
Housewife (Husband's earnings £20. p.w.)

In what way does applicant live according to white standards?
Lives according to normal white standards

What type of dwelling do applicant and family occupy?
Stone 6 rm cottage furnished in normal manner.

Do you consider the applicant is reasonably capable of managing his/her own affairs? YES

Do you consider the applicant is reasonably capable of maintaining his/her family? YES

PLACE: Derby
DATE: 20.10.58
[signature]
PROTECTOR OF NATIVES

18/11/58 SO

C.N.W. Copy has been handed to the Clerk of Courts, Derby as requested in your memo NW/714/48 of 16.10.58 [signature] D.O.N. 23/10/58

Report on Alice Webb's (born Spratt) citizenship application, 28 October 1958.

When Mother's application was refused, my stepfather wrote a letter to the authorities. His letter showed me how much he loved and cared for my mother.

In part, he wrote:

S. J. Webb
Fossil Downs Sth
West Kimberley WA
12 Aug. 1958

Dear Sir,

I am writing to you re: a claim of maternity allowance I made on behalf of my wife, Alice Ethel Webb for our newly born son Richard George.

The Director of Social Services informs me that we are not entitled to the benefit because of my wife's caste.

I am white, British and a tradesman and have always paid my taxation. But on receiving word that we cannot claim for benefit I consider it is worthless for me to pay taxation if I am not going to receive full Social Benefits when the occasion arises.

I am writing now to ask advise [sic] of my wife's position for the future.

Is it possible to get a Certificate of Exemption for her and if not could you furnish full details to Office Citizen Rights.

Since I have known her she has been a good mother and wife and is absolutely honest.

Her education is as good as mine, and I consider mine a good average.

As regards person to vouch for her in the above, I could name a dozen here without the slightest hesitation...

Yours Faithfully

S. J. Webb

Letter from Stanley Webb to the Commission of Native Welfare, Perth, 12 August 1958.

I now call him 'Dad', the only man I have ever called Dad. He came from Bristol, England, which explains his fair complexion. He came to Australia on a boat and got off at Fremantle. Apart from that, I don't know much about Dad's life, and it's too late to talk to him now because he passed away in 2013.

Me and Debbie sang at his graveside after the funeral. Everyone was moved because we sang 'If We Ever Meet Again This Side of Heaven' in harmony as they laid him to rest in the red earth, near our mother, under a beautiful shady tree.

On 13 February 2008, Aboriginal people all across Australia were deeply moved and in tears. The Prime Minister of the time, Kevin Rudd, had finally apologised to the Stolen Generations and said 'sorry' on behalf of the government. His speech came more than a decade after the federal government's *Bringing Them Home* report — also known as the 'Stolen Children' report — of May 1997 that was a milestone in the 1990s, sometimes called the 'Reconciliation decade' in Australia.[4]

I was lucky to go to Canberra and hear Prime Minister Rudd deliver his historic Apology speech.[5] This was possible only through the generosity of a dear friend who wanted to be there, and didn't want to go alone.

The day before the Apology, we flew into Canberra, arriving early evening. Walking on this land, in my heart and mind I sent a silent acknowledgment to the ancestors. I came with honour and a deep respect for them, their sacred lands, and their living descendants.

Walking through the airport, we saw many of our people from all around Australia who had journeyed from near and far to be here on this day. The atmosphere was buzzing. We reached our accommodation a long way out of town, and went to bed with great anticipation in our minds, wondering about tomorrow.

We woke to a beautiful sunny morning, packed our bags and rang a taxi to take us to the Australian Parliament House. What a sight greeted us! Our Aboriginal flags — the red, yellow and black — were flying everywhere you looked. This gave me emu bumps. I felt proud to see so many of our people in one place. That day, we were the majority, not the minority. Mixed emotions filled me as we wandered through the crowd: excitement, sadness, eagerness, happiness, teariness, laughter. Some people were deep in conversation; others shared hugs.

Then, out of the blue, someone called my name.

'Hey! Rhonda Spratt! Is that you?'

I turned and couldn't believe my eyes. Standing there were Peter and Patrick, Beverley Pickett's brothers who I hadn't seen since leaving the mission in 1967. We still recognised each other after all this time. We hugged, had a good yarn about the mission days, and caught up on news about our lives. For me, that made the day even more special — knowing that other mission family was there.

My friend and I stood in line to enter Parliament House. The line was long, and I feared we may not get in. But we did. We were directed to the Great Hall. It was a huge space with polished wooden floors.

When we took our seats, we found that we were in a row with family and friends from Carnarvon. All us Yamatji were together. We held hands and watched the Apology on a large screen. Many tears flowed. My thoughts went to my sister, Debbie, my mother, my grandmother Edna Ronan, my grandfather Clarrie Spratt, my great-grandmothers Alice Ronan and Nellie Spratt, and all the Carnarvon mission kids.

In part, Prime Minister Rudd said in his speech:[6]

> *The time has now come for the nation to turn a new page in Australia's history by righting the wrongs of the past and so moving forward with confidence to the future.*
>
> *We apologise for the laws and policies of successive Parliaments and governments that have inflicted profound grief, suffering and loss on these our fellow Australians.*
>
> *We apologise especially for the removal of Aboriginal and Torres Strait Islander children from their families, their communities and their Country.*
>
> *For the pain, suffering and hurt of these Stolen Generations, their descendants and for their families left behind, we say sorry.*
>
> *To the mothers and the fathers, the brothers and the sisters, for the breaking up of families and communities, we say sorry.*
>
> *And for the indignity and degradation thus inflicted on a proud people and a proud culture, we say sorry.*

When we came outside, me and my friend shook hands with former Prime Minister, Paul Keating. We also met Uncle Bobby Randall, the legendary singer who wrote the song for us stolen children. We mingled with the crowd, and sat on the lawn, yarning with Carnarvon friends, and listening to bands play.

We stayed there for some time, soaking up the atmosphere. At sundown, we made our way to the old Parliament House and the Aboriginal Tent Embassy. We sat around the sacred fire, feeling its warmth. I stared into the orange-red flames, lost in my thoughts.

As the fire flickered and danced with wood and smoke, I thought of our ancestors who sat by their campfires every night, sharing stories about their day. I thought of the many protests that had taken place right here in front of old Parliament House, and of our Aboriginal people who stood strong with courage and strength in front of the brutal, white police line over and over again, fighting for our land rights and human rights — our birth rights — housing, education and health care.

Emerging from my trance, I cleansed my body and spirit with the smoke from the sacred fire. Tents were everywhere because people were sleeping here. A food tent provided a hot cup of tea and a slice of damper with Golden Syrup. Music fused ancient didgeridoo and clapsticks with modern drums and guitar. After a feed, I got up and danced to this deadly music. I danced and danced alone, as if hypnotised, feeling at peace on this spiritual ground. Although it was not my tribal Country, I felt a sense of belonging. This meeting place is sacred to all Aboriginal people of Australia, our own embassy.

For me, the Apology was a necessary act. It was both needed and long overdue. I thank Kevin Rudd for having the courage to say sorry on behalf of the Australian government. For me, it was a stepping stone in my own healing. Hearing Kevin Rudd's words acknowledging the wrongs of the past — the wrongs perpetrated on us as people — the many devastating policies that had affected every part of our lives from who we lived with and where, to the language we spoke, to who we married, to where we worked, to having our wages stolen, and the list goes on — made me feel a release.

It felt good to hear a leading non-Indigenous person, the Prime Minister, state what had happened, admit it was wrong, and say that it should never happen again.

But the Apology didn't happen without some hostility. Many white Australians said that they were against saying sorry. 'I wasn't there,' they said. 'I had nothing to do with the past, so why should I say sorry?'

My understanding is that the Apology was not saying sorry on behalf of the white population. The government was saying sorry to Black Australia for what governments of the past and present had done to us, a nation of Aboriginal people.

Imagine if the shoe was on the other foot. How would white Australians react to losing their children and never seeing them again? Imagine the deep grief, the emptiness after being removed from your mother and your homelands, forced to speak a new language, taught a new way of living and thinking, growing up without any love, told you are a savage, told everything about you is wrong.

I am fourth generation stolen. Me, my mother Alice, my mother's mother and father (Edna and Clarrie Spratt), and my grandfather Clarrie's mother, my great-grandmother Nellie Male, who was born on Liveringa Station, were all taken. Today, Gina Rinehart, a major Australian mining magnate, owns half of that cattle station.[7]

The past is always present, even if you don't want it to be. It controls your thinking and your actions. The past has made me the person I am today with my many faults and strengths. I like to think that I carry the determination and strong spirit of my mother, my grandmother and my great-grandmother.

My sister Debbie who never shows her sorrow, always shows the world her strong side (even though I know her heart is as soft as butter), told me that she watched the apology on TV in her lounge room in Broome. She said she wept for the first time in her life. She told me she thought of our mother and all our family who grew up on missions. The Apology was a way for her to start to let go of the tears she'd been holding on to for so long.

My heart grows heavy, thinking of all Debbie has lived through. I love my little sister very much, and wish I could take away all her sorrows, anger and pain, and throw them into the deepest ocean. There they could turn into beautiful black and white pearls. Her heart would fill with love, her spirit with harmony, her mind with peace, and her life with comfort and calmness.

Sorry Day is now an annual event across Australia, celebrated on 26 May. It's a time to remember the mistreatment of Australia's Aboriginal population. It is a day of coming together, as both black and white, to acknowledge and remember the Stolen Generations, discrimination, displacement from native lands, and forced assimilation of Aboriginal people. Sorry Day allows all Australians to gather as one people. It's a chance for politicians, policy makers and the public to learn more about the ongoing effects that these policies have had on the children who were taken, and on their families and communities.

We are still here in spite of what was done to us and our ancestors. Even to be recognised as part of this nation has been a struggle, and I don't know if I am yet in a place of forgiveness.

11

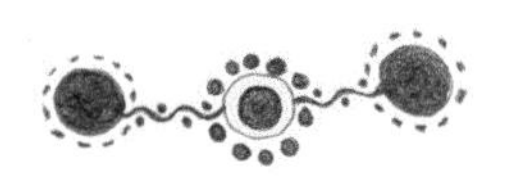

Finding identity

Life in Queensland has been a journey of discovery and healing for me. During the 1990s, government policies finally began to recognise Aboriginal people's right to keep their identity.

In 1994, the government offered me the chance to do a six-week course in Aboriginal art. It changed my life. I found another way of connecting with my culture through creativity. Using the colours of the land, the sea and rainbows, I connected with other Aboriginal people, my Country, language, animals and, most of all, my Aboriginal spirituality.

When I'm painting, I lose track of time; it's like being in a trance. Sometimes, it's like a didgeridoo is playing. I'm totally immersed in the artwork, and feel a strong spiritual connection to the piece. All of my painting comes from my heart. I don't need photos in front of me — visions of what I must paint come to me. It's like the old people, even the birds, are talking to me. Sometimes, I call back to them.

In this painting course, they showed us how to paint on canvas. At school growing up, we'd only used watercolours on paper. Here too, Aboriginal artists were both teachers and students. Because the course was so successful, it lasted longer than six weeks. When it finally finished, I went on to complete an art course at Southbank College.

Then I attended the Queensland College of Art at Griffith University where I learnt photography, gold- and silver-smithing, art history and film-making. Like a sponge, I wanted to soak up all knowledge possible. When I graduated in 2001, I received an award for the best Aboriginal graduating student. It was the first time a visual artist had won that award.

Painting has given me a stronger sense of myself as an Aboriginal person. I now know that I belong to this land. I know what town or city I'm in by the bird calls. In Brisbane, it's the kookaburras and magpies; in Perth, it's the black cockatoos; at Kalbarri, it's the pink and grey galahs. In Queensland, you can hear the mopoke. I lie down and listen for him to call out at night. In one of our legends, he cares for you while you sleep.

Music and my guitar play an important part in my life. They bring me great joy, and give me much comfort. My guitar is my friend. My salty tears have dropped on it, I've written all my songs on it, and I've let my friends and family play it, so now their energy is in it. The memories it holds for me are precious.

Here in Ipswich, in 1995 we formed a band called Black Ochre. We sang country, rock and roll, Aboriginal songs and gospel. But we lost some of the members, and others moved away.

I have now joined a Stolen Generations choir in Brisbane. We go by the name Meanjin Voices, which means the voice of the river. This mix of black and white faces, connected by our love for music, sings both political and contemporary songs.

Music is very powerful because it touches your heart and speaks to your spirit. Music can make you feel happy or sad, it helps bring back memories, and it crosses cultural barriers. Music is the language of the world. Music has helped me on my healing journey, and writing songs is my passion. I write about my experiences, and my mission brothers and sisters can relate to them.

Somebody told me once that all my songs are political.

'Well, that's what it is,' I agreed. 'Being black is political.'

All that I've gone through was created by the government. People will sit and listen to a song. Sometimes, if you are aggressive, people close down. But if you put it into a song, you can get your message across, and people will hear your words.

I still enjoy singing Christian songs, even though I'm not one. These songs bring back memories of the mission, and especially of the kids who grew up with me. Us mission kids have a bond that's there for life, and this music is a part of that.

As a child, dancing was my love. I've carried this love throughout my adult life with jazz, tap, ballet and especially Aboriginal dance. In the mid-1980s in Perth, they held dance classes for our Aboriginal kids at the Aboriginal Centre in Beaufort Street. My son John and me joined this dance group, which eventually became the Aboriginal Dance Development Unit (ADDU). Our dance course was accredited through the Western Australian Academy of Performing Arts (WAAPA).

After a while though we pulled out because our Aboriginal children's bodies didn't fit the typical shape of what they thought a dancer should look like. Our children had shorter, sturdier frames. In our culture, everyone and every body shape is accepted.

My first ballet class brings back a few smiles. In came this tall white man, walking like a penguin, wearing tights with a huge bulge. Being the oldest, I should have controlled myself, but I just busted out laughing. He was good about it and told us to laugh and get it out of our systems. We all started tearing ourselves laughing. Maybe it was the first time he'd taught Aboriginal people. After a while, we settled down and started warming up.

Then we went down on the floor on our backs. When he lay down, the bulge got us all laughing again. That was my first ballet class, but the ballet positions I taught myself at the mission soon came back to me.

In Ipswich, a decade later, while walking down the street, I noticed a poster about belly-dancing in a shop window. I rang the number, and that's how I started belly-dancing. This form of dance is special:

the costumes, makeup, jewellery, the whole package, not to mention the many dear friends I have made. It's a place just for women, and you don't have to be bony.

I first met my dancing friend, Sharron Lindh, at a healing camp for Stolen Generation survivors. We connected straightaway. I call her Emu Girl because the emu is her totem. She calls me Aunt Curlew because the curlew is my totem. We eventually teamed up and created our own style, combining belly-dancing with Aboriginal dance moves, using contemporary Aboriginal music. Sharron and I have danced for NAIDOC Week, Musgrave Park events in Brisbane and women's group events. The joy you see in the women's faces as they dance is beautiful. We share our costumes and our jingly hip scarfs with them, and the women really enjoy trying them on and moving to the music.

One weekend, our belly-dancing group drove out to Springsure in western Queensland to hold workshops. We all travelled together in a small bus. Off in a paddock, in the distance, stood these brolgas.

'Stop the bus! Stop the bus!' I sang out.

'What's the matter, Aunty? Are you all right?' the others asked.

The bus finally pulled over. Looking across the field to the brolgas, I started with the brolga dance. My arms moved like wings, and my feet leapt into the air as I called out 'brrrrrrrp! brrrrrp!', the brolga call.

The brolgas could see me doing their dance and they immediately joined in, hopping gracefully into the air and flapping their wings. Even some of the girls joined me. It felt real good doing the brolga dance. I was reminded of the words of an elder who once told me, 'When you do any corroboree dance of an animal, you must become the spirit of the animal that you are dancing.'

Teaching Aboriginal dance is my favourite work. It brings happiness, and it keeps my culture alive.

Dance with me

I dance in the mist of dawn
Morning Star slowly fades
Sunlight soft, hazy and dim
Creeping quietly into the fresh day
The scent of the land flows through me
My feet hug the cold, damp ground
Dancing to the rhythm of the earth
Her heartbeat speaks to my soul
Her voice I hear singing through the land
Music of the birds lingers in the sky
My feet move lightly on her dusty skin
Swaying, jumping, leaping, stamping,
Dance my child, dance my flesh and blood
Dance with the brolgas waiting for you
Dance with your spirit strong and true
Let your soul feel the ancient embrace
That's always there waiting just for you
Of your mother, sweet mother earth.

Aboriginal land is my only home and the essence of me. My family and ancestors are woven into the land, the sea, the rivers, the rocks, the wildflowers and the sky. This strong connection can never be destroyed, no matter what the Australian government tries to do.

Removing us from family, Country and culture, and trying to extinguish Native Title, have only made us stronger and more determined to survive, and to nurture and protect what we have: our stories, humour, songs, dances, art, land and spirituality. When I'm doing my art, the ancestors and my own family connect with me. My mother was an artist, and my uncles and aunties are artists too.

Before painting, or writing songs, I wrote poetry. My poems reflect my feelings and what I've seen. I remember once lying on a jetty beside the Swan River with Jerry, Lisa and John, watching jellyfish float by. I imagined that the jellyfish were ballerinas drifting past. Poetry is a way of recording the world around you, and the feelings you experience in that world.

Many of my poems are sad, but I find poetry can release pain. Putting feelings into words, on paper, helps you deal with a lot of the hurt you've experienced. For me, that's a good thing. Instead of keeping it locked inside, it helps make the load a little lighter.

Poems are like journeys that you can share with people who might be able to relate to them. A poem might relate to a reader's life. They might learn from it, or feel comforted by it. Poetry is how I deal with a lot of my pain rather than turning to drugs or alcohol. For me, this works. Whatever you put down, nothing's right or wrong. It's how you feel in that moment. It's a safe way of letting go.

Watching

I sit here alone with remote in hand
Thoughts go back to days when we walked this land
Told campfire stories
Beneath the Milky Way and the moon

We heard of the emu who lives in the sky
Sand drawings taught our lore
Songs, laughter and stories fill my mind
Of times long ago, coming back to belong

Chase goanna, look for bardi, bimba too
Chase emus, look for their eggs
Scent of the wildflower fills the red hot land
Slip and slide in sticky mud claypans
Skinny black girls' fun
Fills the remote warm air

Swim in the fresh river water, climb river gums
And lie in the sun
Ochres red, yellow, black and white
Get ready to dance

Oh sweet memory, take me back in time
To a place of peace that once was mine
I'm here alone watching TV
with remote in hand.

12

Through Yamatji eyes

Carnarvon lies on Australia's west coast where the Gascoyne River meets the Indian Ocean and where the wildflowers bloom each spring. It is above the twenty-sixth parallel, about 900 kilometres north of Perth. The region is semi-desert. This place is Ingada Country and is known as Gwoonwardu.

The first mission reunion was held in 2007, and was organised by the Wangka Maya Pilbara Aboriginal Language Centre, together with the Carnarvon Aboriginal Medical Service, Yorgum Aboriginal Corporation, Wangka Maya Link Up and past mission residents.

I wanted to go to this reunion because, over the years, I'd often wondered what had happened to my mission brothers and sisters. Many I had not seen or heard from since the 1960s, but their names, faces and memories were carried in my heart and mind always. We share the same time, same history and same stories. Still, the thought persisted: Will anyone recognise me after all this time?

With my suitcase and guitar, I flew from Brisbane to Perth, then up to Carnarvon. When the plane landed, how great it felt, walking on home soil again. Carnarvon isn't my tribal or traditional Country, but it is the place of my birth, and where I grew up. My emotions and spirit connect me to this beautiful land and to the people who call it home — this land holds my childhood memories.

As I entered the airport, people called out my name. Roslyn Flanagan, married name Kelly, and Irene and Laurie 'Rat' Tittum all greeted me. My heart felt good as I hugged my mission family.

Roslyn still has her nice chocolate Yamatji skin, short dark hair and round face like mine. She still enjoys a good laugh, a yarn and a joke, and remains a very close friend. Irene and I picked up where we left off, and I feel like I've always known Laurie as part of my mission family. After leaving the mission, Laurie worked as a stockman with cattle and horses. He dresses cowboy style and has a beard, which he plaits.

My mother's sister, Aunty Carmel Bellotti, and my cousin sister, Camille Thorne, were also there. Debbie and me would be staying at Camille's home. How lucky to be embraced by my blood family again, to see their faces and mannerisms that reflect my own image and ways. We caught up on family news, and sat in a circle, yarning, laughing, playing guitar, singing songs and enjoying each other's company. It filled my spirit, being home again with my own family who love me just the way I am.

'We miss you and Debbie,' they said. 'And we sure miss your laugh, Rhonda.'

Reunion activities, held at the Gwoonwardu Mia Gascoyne Aboriginal Centre, included weaving, a yarning circle, a group visit to the mission, a barbecue, and a slideshow of old mission photos. The band Red Ochre would play for us on the final night.

On Sunday, they held a morning church service at the Churches of Christ Christian Centre. Although I'd vowed never to set foot in a church again, I was curious to see inside. Many of the mission boys had helped to build this centre. Us mission kids sat together: Tommy Jones, Aunty May Foley, Roslyn Flanagan, Irene Tittums and me. We noticed there too some of the white missionary families who we remembered.

This church that I'd sat in for many years was still the same. Nothing had changed. The only change was the people and the songs.

We didn't know any of the songs, so none of us sang. We were all very emotional, sitting in that church. Many memories came flooding back, and we couldn't hold our tears.

Us mission kids walked out of the service into the foyer, held each other in a group hug, and cried together.

Next day was the mission-site visit. Debbie was in a wild mood. She told me that if a particular missionary man showed up, she would smash him because she hated him. I don't know what this man had done to her, but she told me once that he'd hung her and other little kindergarten kids on the clothesline, pegged up by their braces, because they had wet their nappies. She'd told me how they all fell asleep hanging on that line. It made me proper sorry to see my sister in this state. Her rage and anger were overwhelming. Anything I offered fell on deaf ears. She wanted revenge.

I felt lost and helpless. I grabbed my phone, walked outside and rang Aunty Carmel. Through cries and sobs, I poured out all my feelings and worries. She listened and heard me. Then she told me that I was the peacemaker of the family, and that I could handle this. Hearing this, and speaking to her, calmed me down.

I walked back into my cousin sister's house. Luckily, no one had seen my meltdown. Not wanting my sister to be in trouble with the police for hitting a missionary man, I decided to take my time getting ready. Everything happened in slow motion to make us miss the bus to the mission. I showered slowly, brushed my teeth slowly, dressed slowly and combed my hair slowly.

My plan worked. We missed the bus. Instead, Debbie and me decided to go downtown. Aunty Carmel drove us to have a look around. While there, we saw the bus with our mission family. They stopped and told us we had missed the mission visit, but invited us to join them for a barbecue lunch at the end of the fascine, near the t-jetty. The fascine, which was once a wooden fence but is now a rock wall, is part of the Gascoyne River — a very beautiful place with a cool sea breeze that always blows.

This barbecue was the only time during the reunion that us mission kids and the Aboriginal workers were alone together. No missionaries came. We sang Slim Dusty songs along to my guitar, and enjoyed the food and each other's company.

After lunch, the workers called us together, and invited people to share their thoughts and feelings. Brother Laurie Tittum stood up and walked to the centre. Bravely, he announced that he wanted to talk about childhood sexual abuse. Me and my sister jumped straight up and stood either side of him to support him. A heavy silence fell over the group. No one wanted to talk about it.

Then one girl spoke up. 'I know who I am. I know my language. I know my Country.'

'Well, maybe you don't need to be here then,' I said. 'Maybe your journey is finished. Perhaps you don't need this healing like many of us do. You fullas know this happened.'

Later, Debbie and I told Laurie, 'I'm so proud of you. It takes so much courage to stand up in front of everyone and to speak the words that you did.'

So that's how the day ended, with this subject still floating around up in the air. I guess, people weren't ready to talk about it. But they should acknowledge what Brother Laurie was trying to say and share with us. He told me later that he needed to 'let the cat out of the bag'.

'I'm sixty years old now and I've been carrying this around all this time,' Laurie said, choking back tears. 'It's a heavy burden.'

He had hoped that him speaking about what he'd suffered might help our other mission brothers and sisters to talk about it.

The final night was a celebration for the mission kids and the whole community. Red Ochre played, and things ended on a high note. Everyone was up dancing. It was great to just get together and wind down. It was happy and sad at the same time because we knew we had to journey back to our own homes.

In 2011, I joined a choir set up through my local Aboriginal health centre. Some time later, they were asked to pick the singer who had the most interest and passion for music. So, together with four other Aboriginal singers from Queensland, I was chosen to go to Uganda to sing. Our choir would raise money for orphans who we would visit and work for there.

It was an exciting time for me. They gave us a CD with all of the songs to learn at home by ourselves, and we met up once a month to practise singing our different parts together. It was fun meeting other people from all around Australia who loved music as much as I did. Frantically, I organised my passport.

When they asked me my nationality, I replied, 'Aboriginal. Nyungar nation, and Nhanda and Watjarri of the Yamatji nation.'

I have never said I was Australian. I have always identified myself in this world as Aboriginal because my identity is my bloodline, family connections and land. The government rejected it. They didn't recognise the true me, and processed me as Australian.

Once my passport was finalised, injections followed. Being a diabetic, I needed many immunisations. Then there were the malaria tablets to take. In Uganda, malaria is the biggest killer. It's a sickness you can get from mosquito bites. More people in Uganda die from malaria than from HIV/AIDS.

We flew from Brisbane straight to Africa. I told myself that, since I would be in the Northern Hemisphere for the first time, I needed to check if the water went down the drain in the opposite direction to home. But I forgot.

We flew over the great Sahara Desert. The beautiful image of this landscape stays with me: miles and miles of rippling golden sands disappearing into deep black hollows, and bright yellow sunlight reflecting off the tops of sandhills. The wind moved the loose sand, dancing with it, this way then that way.

Landing in Ethiopia was fun for me because, when our kids were growing up, I'd test them on their general knowledge. My favourite question was, 'What is the capital of Ethiopia?'

They would both shout back, 'Addis Ababa!'

The rhyme and rhythm of this name drew me in. And now I was here, even though we were only at the airport. Never in a million years did I think I would actually get here.

Later that day, we reached Uganda, our destination. The weather was nice and warm, and it continued like this for the whole time we were there. As we rode by bus into Kampala, the capital city, you could see the poverty all around. People on our bus were stunned. It was a culture shock for them, but for me this scene wasn't new. Many of our Aboriginal communities back home live in this same poverty.

Because Britain had colonised Uganda, the people there speak very good English, and it is their official national language. But they also speak their own native tongue, which can be heard everywhere. It is strong and alive, and it was great to hear. I wish I could speak my native lingo fluently, but I can't. My dream is to reclaim my native words.

In Uganda, there's no welfare system to help people out, and it is a male-dominated society. I didn't know what this really meant until I saw it in action. Many women work hard in the fields in the scorching sun. They carry heavy loads on their heads, like large bunches of bananas and big stacks of firewood. Many men stand on road corners, socialising. They smoke, yarn and laugh, passing the time of day in cool, shady places. Some even sleep the day away on their motorbikes. Seeing this made me feel sorry for the hard-working women. Their hot work seemed never done.

Our tour took us to Parliament House. The tour guide explained that if any of us married a Ugandan man, we would have to serve him his meals first, kneeling at his feet with our heads bowed, and holding a plate of food up to him. Most of us women there told our guide we would never do this for any man. We explained to him that this doesn't happen in Australia.

After the city tour, they drove us out of town. We walked on a faded track down a grassy hill to a lonely place, a prison where ex-president Idi Amin tortured many of his own people. Approaching this shady place, I felt a heaviness around me. As we neared the prison entrance, we could see marks where thick spurts of blood had spattered the cold concrete walls of the cells. It was wet and very cold in that dark miserable dungeon.

I tried to enter this killing place to see deep into the rooms, but my feet wouldn't take another step. My guts dropped, and despair overwhelmed me. As I returned outside to the bright, warm sunshine I thought of all the people who were massacred here, and of their loved ones, and wondered whether the perpetrators were ever brought to justice for these crimes against humanity.

The main purpose of this trip was to bring music to three orphanages, and to help build a classroom for the children, paint walls, garden, fix broken-down fences, create two murals and build a soccer pitch. While working, some of the Africans asked me about Australia, so I shared a little of my life story. I talked of black deaths in custody, stolen wages, stolen children. I told them how the cops had threatened to blow my head off and how our people are overflowing in jails. These are some of the many issues we face as Aboriginal people living in Australia, the so-called 'Lucky Country'. This conversation then moved to the back of my mind.

At the first orphanage, we helped with the babies. When we walked into that room, and I saw the rows of little beds and cots, a lump rose in my throat. No choir members knew of my feelings, and no one guessed that I wasn't coping. But tears welled in my eyes, and my emotions were right on the edge. Breaking down was not an option, so I held it together as I always had. Once inside, we saw many precious babies sitting on the floor. We joined them there, cuddling and playing with them.

One little boy crawled over and fell asleep in my lap. The African worker told me that this little boy never went to anyone, so I must have a magic touch. Holding him in my arms, I thought of his mother and father who had both died of AIDS. My heart wished him a good life with enough food to survive, and clean water to drink, and I wished him love.

We fed the babies lunch, bathed and dressed them, then placed them in cots for their afternoon sleep.

We then walked over to where they were building the new classrooms. All us choir mob joined in, laying the cement and passing the bricks with the Ugandan men. We were a factory line, working together to build this much-needed schoolroom.

The choir people had also arranged for us to run workshops for the orphaned children. My workshops included sharing our Aboriginal culture through painting, dance and Dreamtime storytelling. Other choir members taught Zumba dancing.

Fred, a Ugandan man with the most beautiful smile I'd ever seen, helped as well. It was an honour and privilege to share our Aboriginal dance, songs and stories with these cute children whose energy was endless. The room, a large hall, was full of laughs, smiling faces, fun and joy from the bottom of the floorboards to the top of the white ceiling — hugging everyone in the room.

Then, someone harshly called my name. In the doorway, stood the lady in charge of the choir. What could she want? I didn't want to leave this happy room. We walked together out into the bright sunshine where she started jarring me up.

'You're so negative!' she yelled. 'Keep your negativity to yourself. Just get over your wages being stolen. Get over the cops putting guns to your head. Get over being a Stolen Generation. Get over your people overflowing in jails. The people will think "what's all the crime you were doing to be put there in the first place!"'

While she ranted, her face inches from mine, a child's sobbing burst from deep within me. Being with these motherless children had brought back some tough memories and jolted me back to my childhood. I was also very homesick for my homelands. Finally, my sad voice spoke.

'This is your history too. It's our shared history. Why can't you accept it?'

With her next breath, she shrieked, 'These people have absolutely nothing! Don't you understand? They have nothing!'

I could see some of the children peeping through the door at us. The woman gave me a gammon hug and was gone.

Now I had to go back into that happy room with a heart filled with pain and my spirit crying within me. Like a good actor, I hid the real me, put on a fake face, and finished performing my show.

While we ate lunch, a group of teenage girls joined us. They stood in the shade of these big trees and started to sing. Their voices were very sweet, singing in harmony.

But I needed to be alone, away from everyone. I moved a few steps away to a bough shed. Sitting and watching this land, I stared away into the distance. She was beautiful, this Ugandan landscape, but the trees were unknown to me, and the scent of the earth and the shape of the animals, river, hills, ground and insects were all strange. Back home, I belong to the land — I am the land and the land is me. Here, I was a foreigner. For the first time in my life, I was a stranger to a land. What an odd feeling it was, being a stranger and a foreigner at the same time.

For a long time I sat, lost deep in my mixed up thoughts, trying to process my feelings about what had happened.

A young girl's voice brought me back to the present. A very pretty Ugandan girl smiled down at me and asked if she could join me. I nodded. Her name was Rosemary. We shared some of our stories. Sadly, she was an orphan. Her parents had both passed away with AIDS. We sat talking and listening to each other.

Out of the blue, I asked her, 'Would you like me to be a mother to you?'

She hugged me. 'Yes.'

Soon, I was proper glad to be back on Aboriginal land again in Australia. Slowly, life settled back into normal. In quiet times, my mind unpacked the new memories that were born in Africa. All over, I had a deadly time, singing and meeting the people of Uganda, such warm loving people.

Then the words of the choir lady came rumbling back: 'These people here in Uganda have absolutely nothing!'

I tossed these words around in my head and thought, This is not true. This is a lie. All she was thinking about was having things, material stuff. To me and my way of thinking, they had everything. They had everything I never had, and most of my race didn't have: their families, their land, their culture, dances and stories, their language, their identity.

Everywhere they looked, Ugandans could see their own image: in the streets, on posters and billboards; the people working in the banks and shops were people the same as them — same skin, same hair. This would give them a feeling of unity, of not being different, of thinking they could grow up to fully participate in and lead their communities, and make something of their lives. It would give them a strong sense of belonging, knowing this was their place. To me, this isn't nothing. To me, this is everything and so much more.

I was invited to go to Africa again the next year, but I declined. The emotional upset had been too much, and I had felt like just a token blackfulla, a Jacky Jacky.

To this day, my new friends in Uganda, including my new 'daughter' and me, keep in touch. This African trip lives on happily in my heart for the songs we sang, the work we did, and the dances, culture and laughs we shared.

Silence

How can we move forward when the silence isn't heard?
We pretend that things are fine when really they aren't

You say to look forward and not to look back
To forget the past is to deny yourself
The pain of the past is staring at you
Don't look away, don't turn your back
It's here in the land, rivers and seas

My voice is a whisper you choose not to hear
My tears I hold so you cannot see
My body is mine and mine alone
My spirit inside bruised and battered
My mind is free to carry me through
My eyes look deep inside your heart
My hands reach out in search of hope

Can we move forward when the silence is heard?

In 2013, after my stepdad Stan's funeral in Derby, I drove back to Broome, heading to a second mission reunion.

I flew from Broome to Port Hedland. This town is covered in red dust from iron ore. It's a port town, and many huge ships wait hungry on the horizon to have their bellies filled with the rich mineral flesh torn from our Mother Earth.

Here I spent a night with my dear childhood school friend, Cheryl Moncrieff, who used to live on the fringes of East Carnarvon. We enjoyed catching up. Cheryl has grown into a beautiful, generous Yamatji woman who now works with children in care. She is proud of her two kids and of her dog, her four-legged kid.

Cheryl told me that my Uncle Harry Spratt, Mother's older brother, was in the old people's home nearby. She drove me there to visit him.

Uncle Harry grew up with Mother in Moore River Native Settlement. Many years ago, I'd asked him what life was like there. He'd told me that it was too painful to think about, let alone talk about.

Uncle Harry always seemed tall to me, with dark skin and smart clothes. In his younger days, he was a lead guitarist and singer in a country and western band. When he was a young man, his hair was black and always well groomed.

I walked into the old people's home and saw many of our people. Some of them looked up, smiled, and started talking Aboriginal languages to me. But, as I don't speak language, I couldn't understand what they were saying or what they needed. Still, I stopped and held their hands. It was all I could do.

Uncle Harry now looked frail. He was quietly spoken and shy. Sitting by my uncle's bedside, I could see that his once shiny, black hair had turned silver. He seemed to drift in and out of being alert. He would be with me one moment, and then drift back into his own private dream world, looking into space.

I leaned towards him. 'Hello, Uncle. It's me, Rhonda Spratt. Do you remember me?'

He slowly moved his head my way. 'Too right. You're my sister Alicy's daughter!'

He rested his head back on the pillow and closed his eyes. I kept talking to him with a soft voice. 'You like Slim Dusty, inney Uncle?'

'Too right!' he smiled.

So began a two-hour session of all the Slim Dusty songs I knew.

'I love you, Uncle,' I said, when it was time for me to go.

He looked up at me and smiled once again. Before leaving, I held his hand and kissed his soft face goodbye.

Next morning, the buses arrived to take us all to the mission reunion. Two buses left Port Hedland, journeying down to Roebourne where we picked up Betty Coppin, Peter Coppin's sister.

Peter wasn't there. A few years earlier, he had been a witness to a death in custody. He went missing before the inquiry. I liked Peter, and I miss him and his cheeky ways.

'Who's next to pick up?' I asked the bus driver.

He told me it was Lynda and Marine James. We were in Yindjibarndi Country. I ducked down in the bus, so they wouldn't see me.

When we stopped, the door flung open, and I jumped out and ran towards them. They nearly knocked the table and chairs over. We called out each other's names and rushed into each other's arms, crying and laughing at the same time. These two sisters have been in my life forever. After leaving the mission, Lynda went on to become a school teacher. She and her husband now train miners in Aboriginal culture. She is a great supporter of Aboriginal rights and of keeping our cultural heritage alive. Lynda is proud today to see that her mission family are all doing well in their chosen work.

Next, we went on to Onslow where Laurie lives. Mission kids I hadn't seen since I left Carnarvon got on here too. Among them were Marjorie Hughes and Anna Hayes. When I saw Marjorie again, it was like nothing had changed, and she remains a loyal friend. Marjorie had always wanted to marry her childhood sweetheart. And she did. Together, Marjorie and her husband now work in the beautiful Karijini National Park in the Pilbara, looking after Country.

We stayed overnight in Onslow. On the new morning, our next stop was Carnarvon. Two busloads of Yamatjis came from the north, and another drove up from the south.

On the way, Marine and me left the bus for a while to pick wildflowers. It reminded me of our childhood. Marine surprised me by giving me the bunch she had picked.

For this second reunion, we camped in a motel, so we were all together. Way back in the old times, this place, East Carnarvon, was known as Yankee Town. It sits on the fringes where all the Aboriginals used to live. My Nana's house was at the back of this place, on The Block.

This time around, many more mission kids who weren't at the first reunion were here, like Hazel and Marshall 'Diamond Face' Kelly, and Jimmy Ranger. Marshall is Nhanda, and we found out during this reunion that we are related through our great-grandparents. These days Marshall, like all the brothers, likes wearing cowboy gear: jeans, cowboy boots and hats, and belts with big buckles. We prayed a lot for Marshall's family during our childhood. He doesn't go to church now, but when he fills out a form, I suppose he would write 'Churches of Christ'.

Beverley Pickett didn't come to either reunion. After leaving the mission, she went on to become a very good dressmaker. Beverley has had many losses in her life. She is more than a close friend, she is a sister to me, and we talk on the phone often.

Sadly, other mission family have passed on, and this leaves me with a very heavy heart. My first love, Ted, died a few years ago. We stayed in touch over the years.

My special story-telling friend, Susan, is also no longer with us. We had a very close bond growing up, always making up games, and we got a few hidings together too. She was softly spoken, and me and her never fought; we were always kind to each other.

Just being together with all us mission family again was a wonderful experience. I felt I belonged here. They know me, and we speak the same language of our shared experience. We sat together in a yarning circle, creating wreaths with beautiful coloured flowers to place on graves at the old cemetery where my Nana Edna and my mother's two young brothers are laid to rest. While there, Uncle Harry's son, Bertie, came to visit me. He'd received word that his father had passed away. What a privilege it had been to spend time with Uncle Harry before he left to go back to the Dreaming.

When we visited the mission, this time it was all burnt down. A bushfire had gone through in January 2013. It was a shock to see. My aunty told me that while she was driving back from the blowholes, she had seen the mission fire in the distance. She said that the smoke of that fire was real strange. It was like a big whirly wind or willy willy. Aboriginal way, we believe these willy willies have spirits in them. As kids, we were scared of them, thinking the spirit would take us up into the sky with them.

Driving up, a big gate announced, 'Keep Out'.

'How come we can't go in?' we all asked.

'Beware of asbestos' the sign said in small writing.

We had lived in asbestos all through our childhoods.

We finally persuaded the driver to open the gate and drive through. We were not allowed to get out of the bus, however, because of the asbestos.

Jimmy insisted. 'This is my home. This is my place. I need to put my feet on this ground!'

We were all backing him too. But the organisers were firm that we couldn't get out because they had a duty of care to us.

We cried, firstly because our childhood home had burnt down and was now just a pile of twisted corrugated iron and ash. We cried too because we weren't allowed to walk on the land, this land that held the memory of our childhood footprints.

It started to rain.

'Look, the old people, our ancestors too are sad and crying,' Aunty May Foley said.

Everything lay in ashes, destroyed. It was a bittersweet reality. The buildings are now all gone, but the memories live on. One of my old mission mates who has since passed on said she went there one time. The place was dead quiet. As she stood still, looking around at the empty dormitories, she could hear babies crying. She said it was overwhelming and she had to leave.

Once we'd driven in and had a look around, we noticed that the dining room and bunkhouse for the Home Boys were still standing, as was Teens Cottage. They had survived the bushfire.

After our little tour, we sat near the old mission school. They had set out stools in a yarning circle. We were asked to share how we were feeling. Within the group this time hung a very heavy mood. People's faces looked down, and we sat in silence for some time, just being in that moment. People were working through their emotions of being here. I spoke up first.

I called out to the sky. 'Mr Stirling! I want you to know!' I screamed into the wind, 'that all of those things that you said would happen in my life, didn't happen!'

I sat back down again.

Silence. But silence is okay.

Then Roslyn spoke. 'We ought to approach the church board to give this land back to us mission kids,' she said. 'Roelands Mission got theirs handed back.'

Silence. The rest of the group weren't ready to share.

I looked around the circle and saw that some were sitting with their heads low, tears rolling down their faces. Here we were as grandparents sitting near the mission schoolyard where, as young kids, we had raced around, climbed trees and looked for bush tucker. We were old people now, visiting our memory place.

I sat in that circle looking around at all of the faces of my family. None of the brothers spoke. Our men need support because they have lost so much. They used to be the hunters and providers. When welfare came in, our women didn't really need our men for tucker because they could buy their meat and what they needed to survive. Many of our men feel lost.[1]

My heart goes out to all the people in that circle that day. It was okay that people didn't share. The time will come when they can open up and release a little of the hurt that marks their faces. It hit me that they couldn't speak, but, having been there myself, I understand. I realise that I have moved on in my healing journey. I have found my voice and can now express my feelings.

My hope is that each member of my mission family finds their voice too one day, so that they can tell their own stories. If they can't talk it, perhaps they can sing it, paint it, dance it or write it.

Everyone's story is important.

All our stories matter.

Yamatji eyes

I am so far from the place I was born
My heart longs to see familiar faces
See my family
Walk through sandhills where sweet wildflowers grow
Talk to childhood friends and remember mission days
I need to feel the ocean breeze
Toss my hair and look for shells on the long lonely beach

I need to feel warm sand beneath my Yamatji feet
Collect pretty stones from where they sleep
Tell stories in the red sand
Run from goon-na beetles after warm summer rains
Watch eagle-hawks soar high
In the noon day sky
Hear crows call, that's music to my ears
See emus sprint across arid land

I am so far from the place I was born
Yet I close my Yamatji eyes and I am home.

Epilogue

Speaking my truth

Flicking through the pages of my distant and near memories, I know that I am a survivor because of the many cruel emotional trials and losses I've had to bear. Due to the white man's policies and treatment of Aboriginal people, I grew up feeling all alone in this world. A child needs to be loved because love is food and nourishment for your soul and emotional wellbeing. We mission kids were starved of this basic human need, and to this day many of us still feel disjointed, dismissed, cheated and disconnected.

My mission brothers and sisters often say that they have this feeling of emptiness, and they cannot show affection. This devastates our relationships, and many members of my mission family have coped by turning to drink or drugs to block the hurt. I don't carry judgement because I understand. Food is my comfort. And we often don't ask for help. No matter what the situation, we try to solve problems in our own way and in our own time. This lack of a loving upbringing is embedded deep in our souls; it's a scar that is impossible to heal or change. What you learn as a child stays with you forever.

Another scar we carry is our lost connection with family. Many times we feel alone and on the outer. I haven't been in any of my family's lives since I was a kid, and I am not physically in their lives today. Because we haven't created shared memories, that bond is missing. I still wonder, Where do I fit? Where do I belong? My greatest regret remains not growing up with them, and especially growing up without my mother.

If we are going to heal, we need to speak our truth, even if it hurts. Please don't say, 'Get over it and move on.' Please don't say, 'I'm tired of hearing this "poor-fulla-black-fulla" story again', or 'Forget the past.' For me to forget the past is like saying 'forget yourself' because your past shapes you into the person you are now.

Many of my mission brothers and sisters say they feel like crying. I tell them, 'It's okay to cry. Give yourself permission. Cry for that little inner child, that scared little mission child. Cry for that mixed up, abused teenager who lives within you.' Let us feel and cry our pain, and grieve our lost families, lost language, lost innocence and dispossession. Let us work through our sorrow by telling the true history of this land. It's my history. It's your history. Let us share, and together find truth, justice, healing and equality.

In 2004, at an Aboriginal medical centre in Ipswich, Muriel Simmons (I nicknamed her Sam) entered my life as my Stolen Generations psychologist. Sam is a New Zealander and her heritage is Irish, German and English. Sam and me had an instant trust and connection. She has a good heart and spirit, and straight up I talked with her about many issues from my life both as a mission kid and an adult. Sam organised art workshops and day trips with our elders into Brisbane. I helped her with the workshops and, over time, I found out she was much like me: an artist, belly dancer, choir singer and guitar player.

One day Sam asked me to sing with her in a new duo. She came up with the name The Water Lily Waifs because, as she always says, 'Waifs we ain't.' She makes me laugh, true. We have performed for International Women's Day, NAIDOC Week and Sorry Day around Brisbane and Ipswich. Our gigs always open with the song 'Yowie, My Brown Skin Baby They Take 'im Away'. The rule of our little singing duo is 'we have no rules'.

During our time together, Sam has seen the ugly face of racism. In my company, she has seen shop workers be rude to me, or just ignore me. This upsets her.

For the second anniversary of the Apology to the Stolen Generations, Sam and me presented to Prime Minister Kevin Rudd an artwork we had painted together. This painting tells the story of Aboriginal history before and after colonisation. I used our symbols, and Sam used mainstream ones. Our friendship and artwork has led to joint art exhibitions, which we fund ourselves. Sam and me entertain the crowd with our favourite songs and, to our surprise, we sell many of our paintings.

Today I live in two spaces: the black world and the white world. With Muriel Sam by my side, I have taken a giant step into the white space and enjoy many positive experiences there. Like many of us, I travel between these two worlds. In our Aboriginal world, we talk different, our world view is different, where it's 'we' and not 'I', and our sense of humour is 'good crazy'. We add the letter 'h' onto words like h-apple, h-ankle and h-elbow. When we do this, we bust out laughing. When we move into the white world, it amazes me how we automatically switch into white mode. We talk flasher, we try not to put 'h' onto the front of words, and we are often the only Aboriginal person in the room. Then we feel like a fish out of water.

Despite this, and despite ongoing discrimination, throughout the years I have met and developed some positive relationships with white people, mainly women. Sam has taken me out and helped me see a world where life is not just the stark black-and-white existence that I once was locked into. I have come to see the world and life in a new, softer light with its many shades of black and white, and countless shades of grey.

I now know that there are many caring white people in this world. This has been a hard lesson that I needed to learn because I have carried this fear and mistrust of them for a lifetime.

In my adult years, living day to day can be hard. But I find a way to get up and face what each day brings. The blood of my ancestral family flows in me, and their warrior spirit is not destroyed. They can take us away from our Country, culture and family, but they cannot break our bloodlines or our spiritual connection to our tribal lands.

I have always found comfort in Mother Nature. When I'm around water, like the ocean or a river, or out in the bush, that is my place of peace and inspiration. That's me giving love to me. This connection and my life experiences have built me into who I am: a strong Aboriginal woman who, though at times feels fragile, has found her voice and identity, and speaks through her music, art, poetry and stories.

What will the future hold for me and my mission brothers and sisters? My wish is that they will all find peace in their minds, and break the chains of injustice that have been holding them prisoner. May their hearts and spirits fly free and soar high like the wedge-tailed eagle. We all have a story to tell, and all stories are important — to share, or not to share, that is your choice.

Before I leave

Before I leave this world
I want to swim in the river again
Feel the cool fresh water
Wash over my tired aching skin
Heal my spirit with love so true
Fill my soul within

See this land dressed in spring
After rain and warm winter winds
Hear birds and the songs they sing
Lay in wildflowers in full bloom
Surrounded by their soft perfume

In my bed of flower and scent
I watch the clouds softly drift by
Bumble bees buzz
Sweet nectar gathered on their knees
From tall blue flowers they can see

Beneath Carnarvon's warm blue skies
Time takes me back to when I was young
I had no voice and I was shy

Down memory lane I walk once again
Taken to places of my childhood days
Memories come alive strong and true
Then fade away to broken misty blue

Back to the past, my journey isn't through
They fall and sink to the bottom of my mind
Where they will rest till the end of time

Before I go let me sit by your side
Tell me your fears hopes and dreams
Let me sing you a song with story and love
Softly and honestly let it speak to your heart
With my dear friend my old guitar

Now take my hand and dance with me
Under the silent midnight sky

When I leave and have gone to rest
To be with my mother in the arms of Mother Earth
Back to our Dreaming forever I'll be
Think of me when the Morning Star shines
Then think of me when the Evening Star rises

Remember me when the wildflowers bloom
For my heart will be happy, my spirit free

This poem is dedicated to my children, John and Lisa Collard. Love you both forever and a day, Mum.

Glossary

A note on the languages used in this book

Many Aboriginal people across Australia use multiple languages as a matter of course and draw on these languages when speaking English. In the same way, the authors have taken words from across the Murchison, Gascoyne and Pilbara regions, and in particular from Ingada (often written Yinggarda), a Carnarvon regional language that is at risk of dying out, Watjarri (often written Wajarri, Murchison region) and Yindjibarndi (Pilbara) languages, as taught to Rhonda by other children at Carnarvon mission.

As most missions included a mix of people from different areas, in some ways these terms can be seen as creating a regional dialect in its own right. Words that neighbouring language groups have in common may, however, be spelled differently, according to the writing system of each language.

Rhonda also uses colloquial terms and phrases from Aboriginal English and Australian English.

In this glossary, any spelling in square brackets indicates the spelling of the word according to the standard writing system for each of these languages.

[bardi]: witchetty grub, an Australian beetle larva that bores into the roots and branches of plants, and is Aboriginal food

billabong: waterhole in a river or creek

[bimba]: gum or chewy tree sap

binyardi [binyarri]: fight

bough shed: shack with a roof and no walls, traditionally covered in branches and leaves

Bulay! Ulliwah!: [**Balay**] Look out! Look out!

bully beef: tinned, corned (cured in brine and boiled) beef

bush tucker: bush food native to Australia and eaten by Aboriginals, or used for medicine

boogine: mudfish

Byay!: Look at me! Aren't I deadly!

cadge: to borrow or beg for things without intending to repay

clapsticks or **clappers:** wooden drumsticks that maintain rhythm with Aboriginal voice chants by the striking of one clapstick on another

claypans: small dents in the land that fill with rain. When the rain is gone, they fill with clay.

coppertail: slender, fast-moving, lizard-eating Australian snakes, usually less than 1 metre long. Although unlikely to cause more than slight discomfort to adults, large coppertails are more dangerous to children.

corroboree: Aboriginal sacred dance festival to celebrate tribal victories, initiations or other events

cousin brother or cousin sister: In Aboriginal culture, some of your first cousins are considered your sisters or brothers. They are called your 'cousin sisters' or 'cousin brothers'.

damper: any unleavened bread or scone, typically cooked on an open fire

deadly: great, strong, solid, good-looking

didgeridoo: a wooden trumpet or 'drone pipe' made from a hollow limb or tree-trunk, and decorated with traditional designs. It is perhaps the best-known Aboriginal musical instrument.

Dolly Varden: brightly patterned, usually flowered, dress with a polonaise overskirt, draped over a separate underskirt. Cakes of this shape are called Dolly Varden cakes.

doublegees: a low-growing herb native to southern Africa, also known as Spiny Emex and Three Corner Jack. Its female flowers have three sharp, rigid spikes. These spikes harden and can lame livestock.

Dreaming (or Dreamtime): religious concept for the Aboriginal story of creation and those places on traditional land where creation spirits and ancestors live. Aboriginal people are connected to the land through their Dreamings. The Dreaming gives meaning to everything in Aboriginal culture; it sets the rules about relationships between people, the land and all things.

fascine: timber retaining wall along the Gascoyne River in Carnarvon built by settlers between 1910 and 1925. This fascine was built to prevent erosion of the riverbanks during floods.

the flat: a flat piece of dirt or ground

gammon: fake

ging: shanghai, i.e. a slingshot or catapult

gogola [gagurla]: wild pear

goon-na (also spelt [gurna]): faeces or poo. A stink beetle is a goon-na beetle. 'Having the goon-nas' means having diarrhoea.

humpy: temporary bush shelter traditionally used by Aboriginal people

iddy-iddy: a particular crawling and burrowing insect

Ingada (also known as [Yinggarda], Ingarra, Ingara, Ingarda, Ingarrah, Inggarda, Inparra, Jinggarda, Kakarakala and Yingkarta): an Aboriginal language from Carnarvon and the Shark Bay Coast between the Gascoyne and Wooramel rivers and inland of Red Hill, West Pilbara. As of 1981, only five known native speakers of Ingada remained. Ingada is classified as a dying language, as the only fluent users (if any) are older than child-bearing age, so it is too late to restore intergenerational transmission through the home.[1]

inney?: isn't that right?; don't you think so?

Jacky Jacky: Aboriginal person who is easily controlled by white people

jarred us all: told us off or growled at us

jijja [jija]: sister

jimmy-john: a big bottle or jug of wine with a handle

Lore Time: a celebration of the collective knowledge or wisdom of Aboriginal traditional culture

meanjin: the river land where Brisbane is located

[milyura]: snake

[moorditj]: Nyungar word for good-looking, strong

munjong: a scatterbrain; someone with no common sense

ngoojidees: bad spirits

Nyungar (or Nyoongar or Noongar): Aboriginal people from the south-west of Western Australia, including Perth, from south of Geraldton on the west coast to Esperance on the south coast. Traditionally, the Nyungar lived from Jurien Bay to the southern coast of Western Australia, and east to Ravensthorpe and Southern Cross.

pannikin: tin mug

rollies: roll-your-own cigarettes

screws: prison guards

slack: weak, as in 'makes me slack or weak'; feeling down or sad

solid: good, same as deadly, as in a person's character, looks or behaviour

song lines (or song cycles): Many Dreaming stories are presented as elaborate song lines. They show a map detailing the landscape, and expressing relationships between the land, the sea and people. Song lines encompass Aboriginal law, culture and spirituality to ensure the continuity of all living things.

Willy willy: a strong, well-formed and long-lived whirlwind. In Aboriginal beliefs, willy willies represent scary spirits. Parents warn their children that if they misbehave, a willy willy will come down and growl at them.

Wongi: Aboriginal people of the Western desert and goldfields

Yamatji (or [Yamaji] in Watjarri language): Aboriginal people from the Murchison and Gascoyne regions, including Carnarvon, in Western Australia. The word means 'man' or 'human being' in Watjarri, but is often used in Aboriginal English to refer to Aboriginal people, perhaps specifically from the Murchison–Gascoyne region.

Bibliography

Articles/Books/Reports

Aisbett, N and J Duffy, , 'Aboriginal tells of police terror', *The West Australian*, Perth, 7 September 1991, n.p.

Australian Institute of Aboriginal and Torres Strait Islander Studies, *Digitised collections: to remove and protect: Western Australia*, Canberra, 2014, viewed 3 February 2017, <http://aiatsis.gov.au/collections/collections-online/digitised-collections/remove-and-protect/western-australia>.

Australian Institute of Aboriginal and Torres Strait Islander Studies, *The little red yellow black book: third edition*, Aboriginal Studies Press, Canberra, 2012.

Australian Law Reform Commission, *Aboriginal societies: the experience of contact; changing policies towards Aboriginal people (ALRC Report 31)*, Sydney, 1986, viewed 29 January 2017, <http://www.alrc.gov.au/publications/3.%20Aboriginal%20Societies%3A%20The%20Experience%20of%20Contact/changing-policies-towards-aboriginal>.

Beresford, Q., *Rob Riley: an Aboriginal leader's quest for justice*, Aboriginal Studies Press, Canberra, 2006.

Commonwealth of Australia, Royal Commission into Aboriginal deaths in custody, *Report of the inquiry into the death of Ronald Mack Ugle*, Canberra, 17 September 1990.

Cunneen, C, *Report commissioned by the national inquiry into racist violence: Aboriginal–police relations in Redfern: with special reference to the 'Police Raid' of 8 February 1990*, Human Rights and Equal Opportunity Commission, Sydney, May 1990.

Department of Agriculture and Food (WA), 'State barrier fence overview', Perth, viewed 1 June 2016, < https://agric.wa.gov.au/n/2514 >.

Department of Community Development (WA), 'Churches of Christ Carnarvon Native Mission' in *Signposts: a guide for children and young people in care in WA from 1920*, Perth, 2004a, viewed 22 April 2013, <http://signposts.cpfs.wa.gov.au/>.

Department of Community Development (WA), 'Norseman Mission' in *Signposts: a guide for children and young people in care in WA from 1920*, Perth, 2004b, viewed 22 April 2013, <http://signposts.cpfs.wa.gov.au/>.

Department of Planning (WA), *Yakanarra Community Layout Plan 2011*, Perth, viewed 10 April 2013, <https://www.planning.wa.gov.au/dop_pub_pdf/Yakanarra_LP1_Amendment_4_Report.pdf>.

Department of Premier and Cabinet (WA), 'Noongar history: a brief summary' in *South West Native Title Settlement*, Perth, May 2016, viewed 19 January 2017,

<https://www.dpc.wa.gov.au/lantu/south-west-native-title-settlement/Pages/Noongar-History---A-Brief-Summary.aspx>.

eScholarship Research Centre, University of Melbourne, 'Department of Aborigines and Fisheries (1909–1920)' in *Find and Connect Web Resource Project*, Melbourne, 2011a, viewed 31 January 2017, <https://www.findandconnect.gov.au/ref/wa/biogs/WE00388b.htm>.

eScholarship Research Centre, University of Melbourne, 'Western Australian Legislation, Aborigines Act Amendment Act 1936 (1936–1964)' in *Find and Connect Web Resource Project*, Melbourne, 2011b, viewed 29 January 2017, <https://www.findandconnect.gov.au/ref/wa/biogs/WE00411b.htm>.

'half-caste girl's death: a poignant deathbed document: allegations concerning the Moore River Settlement which seem to call for some investigation', *Truth*, 5 September 1925, n.p.

Human Rights and Equal Opportunity Commission (HREOC), *Bringing them home: report of the national inquiry into the separation of Aboriginal and Torres Strait Islander children from their families*, Human Rights and Equal Opportunity Commission, Sydney, 1997, viewed 29 January 2017, <http://www.humanrights.gov.au/publications/bringing-them-home-report-1997>.

Kerin, L, 'National protests planned against closure of WA communities' [audio file], in *The World Today*, 1 May 2015, viewed 1 June 2016, <http://www.abc.net.au/worldtoday/content/2015/s4227459.htm>.

Lewis, M, M Paul, GF Simons and CD Fennig (eds), *Ethnologue: languages of the world, seventeenth edition,* SIL International, Dallas, Texas, 2013.

'On the Fitzroy River', *The Western Mail*, Western Australia, 4 January 1902, viewed 10 August 2013, p. 25, <http://trove.nla.gov.au/newspaper/article/37795910>.

Parliamentary Commissioner for Administrative Investigations (Ombudsman WA), *Findings on an investigation into police conduct: complaint number 21840 — Mrs Rhonda June Collard and Mr Frank Joseph Nannup and the Western Australia Police Department,* Perth, 1994.

Pilkington, D. G., *Follow the rabbit-proof fence,* University of Queensland Press, Brisbane, 1996.

'Police Upstage Theatre in Real Life Drama', *The West Australian*, Perth, 10 September 1991, p. 2.

Randall, B., *Songman: the story of an Aboriginal elder of Uluru*, ABC Books, Sydney, 2003.

Rooney, B, 'The legacy of the late Edward Mippy: an ethnographic biography', PhD thesis, Curtin University, March 2002.

Rudd, K (Prime Minister of Australia), *Apology to Australia's Indigenous Peoples* [audio and transcript], Canberra, February 2008, viewed 18 March 2015, <http://www.australia.gov.au/about-australia/our-country/our-people/apology-to-australias-indigenous-peoples>.

Vidot, A., 'Another boost to WA cattle industry as Rinehart invests' [audio file and transcript], *PM*, ABC News, 2 July 2014, viewed 6 June 2016, <http://www.abc.net.au/pm/content/2014/s4037894.htm>.

Walley, R., *Munjong* [drama], 1990.

Wangka Maya Pilbara Aboriginal Language Centre (WMPALC), *Pilbara history and culture*, Port Headland, 2008, viewed 20 April 2013, <http://www.wangkamaya.org.au/pilbara-history-and-culture>.

Documents

Acting Commissioner of Native Welfare, *Letter to Mr ST Webb, northern district office,* Derby, 25 August 1958.

Court, R (W.A. Liberal Leader). *News Release: Collards to be complemented [sic] on dignity over encounter*, Office of the WA Liberal Leader, 8 September 1991.

Currie, S (Superintendent, Moore River Native Settlement), *Memo to the Commissioner of Native Affairs, Perth,* 16 September 1948.

Currie, S (Superintendent, Moore River Native Settlement), *Record of punishment inflicted, Moore River Native Settlement,* Mogumber, stamped 9 June 1948.

Department of Native Welfare (WA), *Girls to Employment letter*, Carnarvon, 21 November 1967.

Department of Native Welfare (WA), *Report on Applicant for Certificate of Citizenship*, Derby, 28 October 1958.

Department of Native Welfare (WA), *Report on Inmate: Rhonda Spratt*, Carnarvon, 1964.

Ethell, AL (Superintendent), *Memo to Commissioner of Native Affairs, re: Alice Spratt – trainee domestic*, 13 September 1949.

'File no. 1/74/21, 369/29, History of Clarrie Spratt', *Western Australian State Government record*, 11 October 1944.

Fleay, R, *Memo to Department of Native Affairs,* Yarrabubba-Leinster Downs Pastoral Company, Perth, 21 April 1950.

McDonald, R (Minister for Native Affairs, WA), *Warrant No. 1235 to the Commissioner of Police and all police officers within the state of Western Australia*, Perth, 30 November 1948.

Middleton, SG (Commissioner of Native Affairs, WA), *Letter to Mr EO Fleay, Yarrabubba station via Meekatharra,* Perth, 4 April 1950.

Middleton, SG (Commissioner of Native Affairs, WA), *Memo to the Commissioner of Police: Smith*, Perth, 8 December 1948.

Middleton, SG (Commissioner of Native Affairs, WA), *Memo to the District Officer, Central & Goldfields District, re: Alice Spratt*, Perth, 24 May 1950.

Order to send Nellie Spratt to Moore River Native Settlement, Perth, 22 April 1925.

Spratt, A, c/o Mrs Fleay, *Letter to Miss Stitfold, with annotation to Mr Lewis*, 3 March 1950.

Webb, S, *Letter to the Commission of Native Welfare*, Perth, 12 August 1952.

Legislation

Aborigines Act 1905 (WA)

Aborigines Act Amendment Act 1936 (Native Administration Act 1936) (WA)

Native (Citizenship Rights) Act 1944 (WA)

Native Welfare Act 1954 (WA)

Constitutional Alteration (Aboriginals) Act 1967 (Commonwealth)

Notes

Please see this link for further details of Western Australian legislation affecting Aboriginal people referred to in the endnotes below: http://aiatsis.gov.au/collections/collections-online/digitised-collections/remove-and-protect/western-australia.

Chapter 1

1. When the British settled Australia, they considered the country uninhabited or *terra nullius*: land without owners. White racial superiority prevailed, and Aboriginal people's rights did not exist under British law, so colonists believed they had the right to settle throughout Australia (Wangka Maya Pilbara Aboriginal Language Centre 2008). In the area that was to become Western Australia, along with the rest of Australia, Aboriginal people were seen as part of the flora and fauna rather than human beings, and for a while the administration of Aboriginal matters was managed by the Western Australian Fisheries Department (1909–1920) (eScholarship Research Centre 2011a). In 1944, the *Native (Citizenship Rights) Act 1944* (WA) did allow for some Western Australian Aboriginal people to apply to become citizens, but with many conditions, including the requirement to renounce their culture, language and contact with family. In 1967, a national Referendum finally recognised Aboriginal people as Australian citizens (WMPALC 2008).
2. Prior to the 1967 Referendum, West Australian Aboriginal people were initially controlled by the *Aborigines Act 1905* (WA), and then by the *Aborigines Act Amendment Act 1936*, also known as the *Native Administration Act 1936* (WA). Under these Acts, which were repealed in 1963, Aboriginal people had to apply to the Chief Protector of Aborigines to marry; they did not have the right to move freely from reserves or missions; and they had neither property rights nor human rights. This time period was marked by similar legislation in other States and Territories, and came to be known as the Protectionist era in Australian Indigenous policy (Australian Institute of Aboriginal and Torres Strait Islander Studies [AIATSIS] 2012, pp. 87–100.).
3. Spratt, A., c/o Mrs Fleay, *Letter to Miss Stitfold, with annotation to Mr Lewis*, 3 March 1950.
4. Churches of Christ Carnarvon Native Mission is about 1000 km north-east of Perth and 20 km outside of Carnarvon. The mission (1945–1986) was run by the Australian Churches of Christ Indigenous Ministries (ACCIM). In 1975, the mission was renamed Ingada Village, the Aboriginal name for the

area (Department of Community Development [WA] 2004a). Many of the mission buildings burned down during bushfires in January 2013.

5. The *Aborigines Act 1905* (WA) also gave the Chief Protector of Aborigines, Mr A.O. Neville, legal guardianship powers over all Aboriginal children aged up to 16 years. The *Native Administration Act 1936* (WA) increased these powers to control 'children' up to the age of 21. This power overrode any parental legal rights. Mr Neville could remove Aboriginal children from their parents or family as he saw fit, and he did. Many children — particularly children of mixed descent — were removed from their parents and placed in white foster homes, missions, orphanages and hostels. After the *Native Welfare Act 1954* (WA) was passed, many children continued to be removed forcibly and with tragic results. These children, now widely known as the Stolen Generations, often never found their way home, and suffered enormous trauma as a result of these removal policies. Aboriginal parents were often not told where their children were, names were changed, or the children told that their parents were dead (WMPALC 2008).

   In 1995, a Commonwealth Government *National Inquiry into the Separation of Aboriginal and Torres Strait Islander Children from Their Families* was conducted by the Human Rights and Equal Opportunity Commission (now known as the Australian Human Rights Commission). Australia-wide, evidence was taken from Indigenous people, government and church representatives, former mission staff, foster and adoptive parents, doctors, health professionals, academics, police and others. The *Bringing them home report*, handed down in 1997, can be accessed online: http://www.humanrights.gov.au/publications/bringing-them-home-report-1997.

   During A.O. Neville's time in office, the Protectionist legislation of the *Aborigines Act 1905* (WA) and amendments was generally used in preference to child welfare legislation to remove Indigenous children. That way, government officials could simply order the removal of Indigenous children without establishing to a court's satisfaction that the child was neglected. However, as Assimilation became the policy of choice, authorities invoked different laws to achieve the same devastating ends, forcibly removing Aboriginal children from their families and communities. So, despite the change from Protectionist policies to Assimilation programs in Western Australia, removals continued, and were often intergenerational (Human Rights & Equal Opportunity Commission [HREOC] 1997).

6. Norseman Mission (1942–1985) was sponsored by ACCIM. Norseman is a small town about 700 km east of Perth. The Mission Superintendent was a Protector of Aborigines, allowing him to determine who could live on the reserve. For years, Aboriginal families lived at the mission, giving the children in care continuous contact with their language and culture. From the mid-1960s, teenagers from Cundeelee and the Goldfields region, as far out as the

Western Desert, came to Norseman Mission for high schooling (Department of Community Development [WA] 2004a).

7. The government-run Moore River Native Settlement opened in 1918 at Mogumber, 50 km south-west of Moora, under the Chief Protector of Aborigines, A.O. Neville. Moore River began as a self-supporting farm settlement for 200 Nyungar people living in camps and around urban centres. It was originally planned to provide health facilities, schooling for children and employment for adults. Chronically under-funded, it became more like a prison for Aboriginal people from all over WA (Rooney 2002). Children of 'mixed descent' were separated from their parents, lived in dormitories, and were trained as domestic servants for white society. The *Little red yellow black book* describes one particularly nasty punishment: 'those thought to be acting badly were placed in "The Boob", a prison within a prison' (2012, p. 94).
8. The rabbit-proof fence is the state barrier fence of Western Australia. Built 1901–1907, it protected the state's pastoral areas from rabbits and other pests. Doris Garimara Pilkington's memoir, *Follow the rabbit-proof fence* (1996) is set in the 1930s. It recounts the story of how three Aboriginal girls who were taken from their parents and placed on Moore River Native Settlement escape and follow the fence to find their way back home to Jiggalong. The 2002 major motion picture *Rabbit-Proof Fence* is based on the book (Department of Agriculture & Food [WA] 2016).

Chapter 2

1. Gogo Cattle Station, also known as Margaret Downs, is a pastoral lease about 10 km south of the township of Fitzroy Crossing in the Kimberley. Established in 1885, Gogo occupied 1,750,000 acres (708,200 hectares) by 1902 ('On the Fitzroy River' 1902). In 1985, 3km^2 was excised from the property to form the Aboriginal community of Yakanarra, home to about 150 Indigenous Australians (Department of Planning 2011).

Chapter 3

1. The origins of assimilation policies in Australia can be traced to a 1937 meeting of State and Commonwealth officials responsible for Aboriginal affairs in Canberra. By the 1950s, assimilation was the well-established policy aim for Aboriginal Australia, adopted by all levels of Government. assimilation, as stated at the 1961 Native Welfare Conference of Federal and State Ministers, meant that in theory 'all Aborigines and part-Aborigines are expected to attain the same manner of living as other Australians and to live as members of a single Australian community ... accepting the same customs and influenced by the same beliefs as other Australians' (Australian

Law Reform Commission 1986) The assimilation project continued well into the 1960s, despite mounting opposition and evidence that assimilation was unsuccessful, including reports on the psychological damage that forced removals caused (HREOC 1997). In 1972, the Commonwealth Government under Prime Minister Gough Whitlam officially abandoned policies of assimilation in favour of self-determination (AIATSIS 2012, pp. 101–102).

2. The 'Native Act' was the popular name for the *Aborigines Act Amendment Act 1936* (also known as the *Native Administration Act 1936* (WA)), which amended the *Aborigines Act 1905* (WA). This act extended the powers of the Chief Protector (now called the Commissioner for Native Affairs) by broadening 'native' to include all Aboriginal people described as of 'full' descent, any descendants 'of less than full blood', including 'half-caste' and 'quadroons' under the age of 21 who lived with other 'natives', or 'lived after the manner of the original full blood inhabitants or their full blood descendants'. (eScholarship Research Centre 2011b).

Chapter 6

1. Kerin, L., 'National protests planned against closure of WA communities' [audio file] in *The World Today*, 1 May 2015.

Chapter 7

1. Perenjori is a town-site in the northern agricultural region, 350 km north-east of Perth.
2. Commonwealth of Australia, Royal Commission into Aboriginal deaths in custody, *Report of the inquiry into the death of Ronald Mack Ugle*, Canberra, 17 September 1990.
3. ibid.
4. Beresford, Q., *Rob Riley: an Aboriginal leader's quest for justice*, Aboriginal Studies Press, Canberra, 2006.
5. Commonwealth of Australia, Royal Commission into Aboriginal deaths in custody, *Report of the inquiry into the death of Ronald Mack Ugle*, Canberra, 17 September 1990.
6. ibid.
7. ibid.
8. ibid.

Chapter 8

1. Walley, R., *Munjong* [drama], 1990.
2. 'Police Upstage Theatre in Real Life Drama' in *The West Australian*, Perth, 10 September 1991, p. 2.

3. Cunneen, C, *Report commissioned by the national inquiry into racist violence: Aboriginal–police relations in Redfern: with special reference to the 'Police Raid' of 8 February 1990,* Human Rights and Equal Opportunity Commission, Sydney, May 1990.
4. Aisbett, N and J Duffy, 'Aboriginal tells of police terror', *The West Australian*, Perth, 7 September 1991, n.p.
5. Parliamentary Commissioner for Administrative Investigations (Ombudsman WA), *Findings on an investigation into police conduct: complaint number 21840 — Mrs Rhonda June Collard and Mr Frank Joseph Nannup and the Western Australia Police Department,* Perth, 1994.
6. ibid.
7. ibid.
8. ibid.
9. 'Police Upstage Theatre in Real Life Drama' in *The West Australian*, Perth, 10 September 1991, p. 2.

Chapter 9

1. 'File no. 1/74/21, 369/29, History of Clarrie Spratt', *Western Australian State Government record*, 11 October 1944.
2. 'half-caste girl's death: a poignant deathbed document: allegations concerning the Moore River Settlement which seem to call for some investigation', *Truth*, 5 September 1925, n.p.
3. 'File no. 1/74/21, 369/29, History of Clarrie Spratt', *Western Australian State Government record*, 11 October 1944.
4. The Chief Protector of Aborigines, A.O. Neville, saw settlements as a way of assimilating children of 'mixed descent' into mainstream non-Indigenous Australia. By physically removing Aboriginal children from their families, educating them in the European way, and training then sending them out for domestic or stock work, he theorised that 'they would be accepted by non-Indigenous people and lose their identification as Indigenous people' (HREOC 1997).
5. Currie, S, (Superintendent, Moore River Native Settlement), *Record of punishment inflicted, Moore River Native Settlement,* Mogumber, stamped 9 June 1948.
6. ibid.
7. McDonald, R (Minister for Native Affairs, WA), *Warrant No. 1235 to the Commissioner of Police and all police officers within the state of Western Australia*, Perth, 30 November 1948.
8. Middleton, SG (Commissioner of Native Affairs, WA), *Memo to the Commissioner of Police: Smith*, Perth, 8 December 1948.
9. Currie, S (Superintendent, Moore River Native Settlement), *Memo to the Commissioner of Native Affairs,* Perth, 16 September 1948.

10. Ethell, AL, (Superintendent), *Memo to Commissioner of Native Affairs, Perth, re: Alice Spratt – trainee domestic*, Perth, 13 September 1949.
11. Middleton, SG (Commissioner of Native Affairs, WA), *Letter to Mr EO Fleay, Yarrabubba station via Meekatharra*, Perth, 4 April 1950.
12. Fleay, R, *Memo to Department of Native Affairs, Perth,* Yarrabubba-Leinster Downs Pastoral Company, 21 April 1950.
13. Middleton, SG (Commissioner of Native Affairs, WA), *Memo to the District Officer, Central & Goldfields District, re: Alice Spratt*, Perth, 24 May 1950.
14. Acting Commissioner of Native Welfare, *Letter to Mr ST Webb, northern district office,* Derby, 25 August 1958.
15. Beresford, Q, *Rob Riley: an Aboriginal leader's quest for justice*, Aboriginal Studies Press, Canberra, 2006.

Chapter 10

1. 'My Brown Skin Baby, They Take 'Im Away' (1970) by singer-songwriter Uncle Bob Randall (1929–2015) focused national and international attention on the Stolen Generations. A documentary of the same name won Bronze at the Cannes Film Festival. Subsequently, the Australian government stopped taking Indigenous children away from their families (Randall 2003).
2. Acting Commissioner of Native Welfare, *Letter to Mr ST Webb, northern district office,* Derby, 25 August 1958.
3. To be free of the control of the *Aborigines Act 1905* (WA), and the subsequent *Aborigines Act Amendment Act 1936* (WA) (also known as the *Native Administration Act 1936* (WA)), Aboriginal people had to gain Australian citizenship under the *Native (Citizenship Rights) Act 1944* (WA). To become a citizen, they completed an application that stated their 'caste' and the 'caste' of their parents, paid a fee, provided a photo and references as to their good character, and 'dissolved tribal and native association' from Aboriginal people and culture. A board then decided if citizenship was approved. Once citizenship was gained, the Chief Protector could remove it at any time (WMPALC 2008).
4. HREOC 1997.
5. Rudd, K. (Prime Minister of Australia), *Apology to Australia's Indigenous Peoples* [speech], Canberra, February 2008.
6. ibid.
7. Anna Vidot, 'Another boost to WA cattle industry as Rinehart invests' [audio file and transcript], *PM*, ABC News, 2 July 2014.

Chapter 12

1. Aboriginal people's traditional mode of socio-economic organisation was hunting and gathering. Although the economy of pastoral Australia was sustained by Aboriginal labour, during colonisation white pastoralists

justified not paying Aboriginal workers a cash wage based on 'poor returns' and 'supposed unreliability'. When the Equal Wages Award was implemented in 1968, pastoralists still refused to pay these wages, and workers were exiled to towns and urban centres without access to traditional foods and lands to practice these important skills (AIATSIS 2012, pp. 95–96).

Glossary

1. Lewis, M, M Paul, GF Simons, and CD Fennig, (eds), *Ethnologue: languages of the world, seventeenth edition,* SIL International, Dallas, Texas, 2013.